The Intelligent Forex Investor

World Currency and World Commodities

Benjamin Graham

For information regarding special discounts for bulk
purchases, please contact BN Publishing at
sales@bnpublishing.net

PREFACE

THE general subject of this study is world planning for raw materials. More particularly, it seeks to develop the possibilities of the reserve or stockpile technique for achieving the goals of expansion and reasonable stability in the postwar economy. The author's chief purpose will be to present and expound a concrete plan directed toward these ends. Thus the book is essentially the application to the international sphere of the proposals he developed in *Storage and Stability*, published in 1937.

Commodity reserves may play a role of importance in three major areas of economic policy. The first, obviously, is the building up of raw-material stockpiles for national safety and well-being. It is natural that current thinking should emphasize the value of such stockpiles in future wars but there are wider and more inspiring uses of a sound commodity-reserve system for the ends of peace.

The second area is that of stabilization—more accurately, the prevention of disruptive short-term swings in the price level of basic raw materials. This aim is a central element in the broader objective of narrowing the trade cycle, avoiding deep depressions, and maintaining high-level employment.

At this point we face what is probably the crucial issue of the postwar economy. It grows out of the seemingly irreconcilable conflict between the two aims of reasonable stability and over-all expansion. In modern business, booms generate depressions, mainly because broad expansion creates commercial oversupply and instability. In the battle of the twentieth century against instability its chief weapon, to date, has been restriction of output and sales. It has sought to cure the evils of plenty by removing the plenty. Unless we can devise a major technical improvement in our economic machinery, the postwar world will return to that unsatisfactory weapon for want of a better. It will preach expansion and practice cartelization.

The third area we invade is that of monetary policy—in particular, the establishment of a sound, adequate, and stable world currency. Here it is most important to build upon what we already have. To the fullest extent possible the monetary uses of gold should be conserved, and the limited currency values inherent in silver should not be rejected. But *in addition to these*, the world can use its basic, durable commodities as monetary reserves. By so doing it can contribute mightily, and at a single stroke, to solving a host of major postwar problems: the promotion of wide expansion; the attainment of reasonable price-level stability; the establishing of useful and nondisruptive stockpiles; the creation of more adequate purchasing power in the hands of farmers and of raw-materials nations; and the facilitating of foreign trade, of trade-balance settlements, and of stable currency values.

These are ambitious claims, but they should not be misconstrued and exaggerated. Other plans and agencies, besides commodity reserves, will be needed to carry out successfully the above objectives. The world will face a host of other problems, both political and economic, toward which commodity reserves will contribute little or no solution.

America's huge stockpile of gold has aroused a complex of emotions, ranging from complacency and pride, through bewilderment, and down to dismay and derision. Perhaps its most useful lesson is that of example. The gold-reserve system has meant stability, expansion, and full employment *for the gold-mining industry*—except in this war, when the world needed much more important things than gold. An analogous reserve system for basic commodities can mean reasonable stability, balanced expansion, and high-level employment for all the primary industries of the world. To this will be added the creation of national reserves which should be at least as useful as gold in peace and immeasurably more valuable than gold in time of war.

While this book was in press, the International Monetary and Financial Conference was held at Bretton Woods, New Hampshire. Surmounting technical difficulties, it produced two agreements, one for a world monetary fund and the other for a world capital bank. The monetary fund follows, in the main, the pattern set forth in the so-called experts' plan, which is discussed in the later chapters of this book.

The author's proposal for an international commodity reserve currency was not on the agenda of the conference, but it has claims on the attention of the commissions which are to continue its studies. Commodity-reserve currency can contribute to the successful operation of the projected International Monetary Fund by remedying elements of weakness which have inspired doubt and criticism. Since it will stabilize the world price level of basic commodities, as well as that of gold, the plan will prevent the rigid gold standard from spreading deflation and depression—as some nations fear—from one part of the world to another. Since it will increase greatly the ability of primary producing nations to pay for goods with goods, it will hold down the credit operations of the IMF within a compass which the export-balance nations should readily accept.

At the monetary conference, raw-materials countries, led by Cuba,* urged that stabilization of commodities be considered along with currency stabilization. This might be accomplished by use of the now familiar International Commodity Agreements, but only at the price of a degree of curtailment and cartelization which the world would be loath to accept. It is the thesis here that the approach should be through buffer stocks rather than through restrictive agreements. In this respect the commodity reserve proposal provides a bridge between the Hot Springs and the Bretton Woods conferences. The food conference stressed the role of buffer stocks of agricultural commodities as a stabilizing

* See *New York Times*, July 26, 1944, p. 1.

factor both in food supplies and in the price structure. It is suggested here that such buffer stocks, expanded to include industrial materials, be incorporated in the international monetary system. By a comparatively simple technique, we could thus achieve the fourfold objective of foreign-exchange stability, reasonable price stability, protective stockpiles, and—most important of all—a balanced expansion of the world's output and consumption of useful goods.

The author's thanks are extended to Mr. Irving Kahn for considerable assistance with the manuscript and the tables, and also to Mr. Louis Bean for helpful suggestions.

Benjamin Graham.

New York City,
September, 1944.

CONTENTS

CONTENTS

Chapter I

THE PROBLEM OF RAW MATERIALS

"It passes the boundaries of sanity when men stand in fear of the good earth's bounty, damned with the epithet 'surplus.'"
—HENRY M. WRISTON, "Challenge to Freedom," p. 15.

THE basic problem of raw materials is how to reconcile stabilization with expansion. Both these aims are of paramount importance; yet they seem to be inherently incompatible. We have, on the one hand, developed many and varied stabilizing measures, but the underlying emphasis of all of them has appeared to fall upon restriction of sales and production. On the other hand, the universally accepted ideal of expanding output has proved amazingly difficult to realize. Only under the stress of wartime demand has it been possible to increase production steadily without bringing on collapse and disruption.

It is the task of the postwar world to resolve this conflict between stability and abundance. It cannot be called easy; it must not be termed impossible. The proof of its possibility lies in the fact that all the economic elements involved are sufficiently within man's control. But were the problem an easy one it would long ago have been overcome. It is clear that the old techniques must be improved upon, that there must be some degree of innovation. Unfortunately innovations in economics are necessarily more suspect than those in other fields. They cannot be tried out experimentally in a laboratory or a pilot plant; if the idea proves impracticable or unsound, a whole nation must suffer the consequence. In economics, therefore, while blueprint inventions are plentiful, it is only necessity that brings any of them to practical birth.

Such necessity confronts those who are to guide the postwar world. The peoples of the earth have been promised a fuller peacetime utilization of its resources, the pattern for which has already been exhibited in the stupendous achievements of war production. Not only must substantially full production be attained after the war; it must be *maintained* as well, without the once familiar aftermath of a pricked bubble and a deep depression. The men and women of tomorrow's world will patiently accept calamities that flow from the harshness of Nature but not from the ineptness of their leaders.

This battle for an acceptable world economy must be fought on a number of fronts. Perhaps the most important of these is the area of raw materials. Raw materials are not only and obviously the blocks from which the economic structure is built, but they are also the "Medicine Hat" in which most of our fiercest economic storms are brewed. The primacy of the raw materials problem is self-evident in the international field. We have no clear concept of world manufacturing, wholesaling, or retailing problems. Money problems are often viewed internationally, but more frequently the proposed solutions have been geared to a specific national situation. However, the important raw-materials difficulties always appear to develop against a background of world trade, and of imbalance between world supply and demand.

The prominence of raw-materials problems in world economic thinking is shown by the emphasis they have received in international discussions ever since First World War. They have been the subject of two formal inquiries by the League of Nations: in 1921 and 1937; as well as of an extensive study carried on by its affiliated Institute in 1939.[1] There has been governmental participation in at least seven peacetime agreements seeking to stabilize world trade in specific commodities. (These covered beef, coffee, rubber, sugar, tea, tin, and wheat.) All these agreements have been related to raw products; no similar cooperative action has been taken by sovereign states in the field of manufactured goods or of services. The Atlantic Charter, in paragraph 4, promises "to further the enjoyment of all States . . . of access, on equal terms, to the trade and raw materials of the world." Here in the foundation stone of the new world order we find specific reference to the basal position of primary commodities.

What are the troubles which the world faces in the field of raw materials, and how do these compare with and affect our other major economic problems?

The various studies of the raw-materials question have mentioned a long list of difficulties, each of which has no doubt done its part to complicate the subject. But the subject may be approached more effectively if we concentrate our attention on three aspects which seem to be of first importance, *viz.*,

1. Inability of poor nations to import and pay for as large amounts of basic commodities as their peoples would like to consume.

2. The instability of raw-materials prices, due (*a*) to an underlying insufficiency of effective demand, and (*b*) to cyclical unbalances between production and consumption.

3. The trade barriers of all sorts imposed by nations against imports, proceeding in part from doctrines of self-sufficiency and economic nationalism.

These three sections of the problem are obviously interrelated, but they lend themselves to separate examination and discussion. The various points might be made clearer from time to time by reference to a single specific commodity. We have selected *coffee* for this purpose, because that comforting product has run perhaps the widest gamut of problems and solutions during the past 40 years.

1. *Inherent Overproduction*

The first of our troubles with raw materials is the simple fact that the world is capable of producing more of them (or of most of them) than can be sold, exported, imported, and consumed. Yet this fact is simple in appearance only. Why should not the world be financially able to consume what it is physically able to produce? If production is purchasing power, as the classical economists assert, the sum total of the commodities produced should always generate enough purchasing power to carry them into consumption. Nor should the fact that some countries are richer than others dislocate this fundamental equation of output and cash income.

The fact that the world does not consume as much coffee as it produces cannot be due to the ingrained poverty of the world. Nor, surely, does it arise from the sated appetite of mankind.[2] The cause must lie elsewhere, first in lack of balanced production among commodities, and second in the world's inability to expand output without breaking the price structure. The coffee crops of Latin America furnish a clearcut case of unbalanced production. Their volume has been far higher than the world could absorb in relation to the production and consumption of all other things, i.e., in relation to its standard of living. Hence, in the case of coffee we have seen that ultimate absurdity of modern economics—the destruction of the earth's bounty—proceeding not only in years of deepest depression but season after season, in good times and bad. From 1931 through 1943, more than 75 million bags were burned; that is over 100 billion pounds, enough to supply the whole world for four years.

Yet if all countries had enjoyed the per capita income of the United States, or even if they had drunk coffee at one-half our per capita rate, the crops of Brazil and the rest of Latin America would have been far less than enough to supply the global demand. Thus it is true, as the conservative economists have always claimed, that the best cure of a specific overproduction lies in a general expansion in all other lines.[3] Coffee has been forced into a kind of economic balance by destruction of its own output; it could theoretically have found a much better balance through the upbuilding of the total output and over-all income of the world. The same statement undoubtedly applies to wheat, sugar, and cotton— the three commodities of major rank which have seemed to be in chronic oversupply during most of the prewar decade.

What has stood in the way of this worldwide expansion on every front? Dozens of answers can be given—lack of money, of capital, of credit, of confidence, of free trade, of peace on earth, and of good will among men. But there is evidently a subtler cause—an obstacle to expansion inherent in the very process of expansion; a certain dependence on speculative and therefore unstable elements; a tendency for commercial inventories to grow and become menacing; and an apparent need for steadily expanding credit, i.e., the creation of an ever-increasing debt. The world has not yet learned the technique of balanced expansion without resultant commercial and financial congestion.

We have indeed succeeded in multiplying our output phenomenally under the impact of war. This achievement has inspired a deep determination among serious thinkers everywhere to attain a similar abundance under conditions of peace. But there are two major differences to be reconciled between war production and peace production. The first is that war goods need only to be made; the goods of peace must be made and sold. The second is that in this war money hardly counts. Whatever a nation needs and can produce it manages to pay for somehow, out of taxes, savings, or inflationary borrowing, and in whatever proportions prove expedient.

Responsible people are not prepared to accept this solution to the problem of maintaining full production and full employment in peacetime—certainly not to the extent of any close approximation to wartime controls and wartime fiscal policy. Whether or not a steady expansion of national debt in moderate amounts should be accepted as an instrument of economic policy remains a hotly controversial question.[4] Certainly the man in the street is mistrustful of the idea that by increasing our debt we can cure our basic ills. In any event, the huge borrowings associated with war efforts are out of the question as a normal and continuous practice.

If this issue be viewed on the world level, rather than as a problem solely for the United States, the objections to uninterrupted budgetary deficits as the source of expanding consumer demand become more decisive. Just who should incur the new debt, and in what amounts, would be the subject of interminable argument. And the ever-mounting total of internal and foreign borrowing could hardly fail to produce new stresses and breakdowns.

Even if money incomes were built up constantly by government spending in peace, as they are in war, the result might not approximate that balanced and steady expansion of production and consumption which is the goal of economic progress. There might still be great irregularities in the spending and saving habits of the people. Also, highly uneven movements in inventory totals and in the demand for capital goods could create cyclical variations of embarrassing magnitude. If the wartime dictation by government of our producing, consuming, and investing activities were carried over into the peace, these particular difficulties might be surmounted. Such regimentation might fail for lack of cooperation or popular support and, even if successful, might seem too high a price to pay for the more abundant life.

Very likely a great deal more of today's war economy will be continued in tomorrow's peace than was true of former conflicts. Governments will use every device of control to prevent both a runaway postwar boom and the conventional postwar depression. The basic means to achieve balanced expansion and reasonably stable business should, if at all possible, be suited to the atmosphere and psychology of peace. As little interference as possible with the individual's economic choices, as close adherence as possible to the accepted canons of sound fiscal policy—these are two self-evident principles which should guide the planners of world peace and prosperity.

The foregoing discussion has not been addressed particularly to raw materials, since insufficiency of purchasing power affects all types of goods and services. But it has been closely relevant to the first of our three main problems of raw commodities, i.e., the difficulty the world finds in buying all of each commodity that it can produce. There should exist effective ways of dealing with this challenge, and their application should prove simpler in the field of basic materials than in that of finished goods, because a relatively few primary commodities underlie a large part of the total economy. What these ways are remains the subject of our later inquiry. So far we have merely pointed out that the easy solution provided by war demands and war financing cannot so readily be imitated under conditions of peace.

2. *Price Instability*

The instability of raw-materials prices is the second aspect of our general problem. In part, at least, it is the obvious consequence of the insufficiency of demand which we have just discussed. But this price instability has characteristics of its own as a source of economic disturbance. If the sole trouble with the world was that it normally consumed 28 million bags of coffee instead of, say, the 35 million bags readily produced we might shake our heads at this perversity, yet it would scarcely carry the threat of crisis and ruin. Price collapses undermine the entire financial structure of business, not only in its ability to make profits, but more important still in its ability to pay its debts.

The chief harm to business in major depressions comes not from ordinary operating deficits but from inventory losses due to severe price declines. The most intense of these are in the field of raw materials. Furthermore, it is this price weakness of primary commodities that antecedes and induces later disrupting declines in the level of finished goods.

Most serious is the effect of price collapses on the position of those countries chiefly dependent on the production and export of raw materials. The reduction of the national income and the impairment of the living standards of the population are catastrophic; defaults on foreign debt, severe reduction in imports of finished merchandise, new trade restrictions, and depreciation of the currency—all these consequences are inevitable.[5] The great need for stabilizing the price of important raw materials, within reasonable limits, is recognized by nearly everyone. The sole question is whether and how this can be done effectively, and without creating new problems of similar magnitude.

We have suggested that one cause of price instability lies in the tendency of production to outrun effective demand. It may be asked why, if this tendency is chronic, we do not have a continuous decline in the price of raw materials, bringing them ever nearer to the vanishing point. The answer, of course, is first that these very price declines bring counter-measures, mainly by governments, looking to curtailment or destruction of output, crop loans, export bounties, etc. In some cases low prices have forced producers out of business; in others, drought, insects, or plant diseases have finally caused crop failures and short supplies. Above all, two world wars have swung the balance temporarily from overabundance to insufficiency.

Next to war demands, the wide gyrations of the business cycle have produced the most significant changes in the price of raw commodities. It is not always easy to separate war influences from peacetime cyclical movements. This is particularly true with respect to the postwar speculative rise of 1919–1920 and the great collapse of 1921–1922. But the even more devastating drop in 1931–1932 and the serious break of 1937–1938 were clearly the products of modern commercial cycles. If we are asked whether commodity price weakness is a cause or a result of business depression, we might first give the obvious answer that such declines are both cause and effect in the progress of the vicious spiral. It would be more exact to point out that in the early stage of a downswing commodity price weakness is more likely to follow as a consequence of other happenings, e.g., a stock market collapse; but after the initial stages, the drop in raw materials prices becomes one of the chief factors that *intensify* the depression.

A new cycle of price instability began in 1939. By the end of 1943 it had produced a rise of 79 per cent in the price level of basic raw materials in the United States.[6] There are dangers of further advances before the war ends, and of a more spectacular—because less controlled—upsurge in the reconstruction period. This includes the possibility, though hardly the likelihood, of an all-out monetary inflation or flight from the dollar.[7] In many other nations the purchasing power of their money has already been ruined; for them an entirely new price level or exchange parity, or both, will have to be constructed when peace comes.

Along with deep-seated fears of a menacing inflation, we find existing in America, serious apprehensions of exactly the opposite import. After reconversion is accomplished and the production of civilian goods hits its stride, many businessmen and economists expect the familiar cyclical process to repeat itself. The combination of somewhat slackened demand, greatly expanded output, and overextended inventories will, they feel, yield the inevitable result of price weakness, serious business depression, and widespread unemployment.

In January, 1944, a highly pessimistic forecast was made by Richard V. Gilbert, economic adviser to the Office of Price Administration. He foresaw a drop of not less than 15 or 20 billion dollars in the purchasing power of workers, arising merely from the elimination of overtime and from shifts in employment from war industries to peace industries. Assuming further a drop of 10 per cent in employment and another 10 per cent in wage rates, he feared a total reduction in purchasing power of between 30 and 35 billions. A cut of this magnitude would constitute a critical threat to our economy.[8]

The National Resources Planning Board warns us that we may witness both prosperity and depression existing side by side. This is their statement:

Today one fact, more than anything else, needs emphasis and reiteration. There are those who think that there will be a boom after the war and those who think there will be a depression. Both are right: *We shall have a boom and a slump simultaneously*. There is every indication that the end of the war will let us in for a "spotty" period, with all the superficial aspects of a boom—inflationary pressure on prices, shortages, attempted

inventory accumulation—at the same time that we shall have all the disadvantages of a depression involving dislocations of manpower and plant,
unemployment, and less than potentially obtainable real income.[9]

The fact that either of these opposite calamities seems
possible and that each is feared by one set or another of
economists might possibly indicate that both can be avoided
by skillful planning and execution. In truth we are dealing in
our modern economy with two powerful forces of contradictory character, the inflationary influence of huge government deficits and the deflationary weight of a technology
that has outstripped our ability for smooth absorption of
its products. These forces may balance themselves out by
sheer accident, but such luck can hardly be hoped for. We
must devise policies, and perhaps new mechanisms, calculated to maintain the inflationary and deflationary elements
in reasonable equilibrium. Those who try this task may
expect to be criticized while they work and condemned if
they fail. The attempt must still be made, for to do nothing
is to risk greater catastrophe.

In sum, therefore, the task of creating a reasonable degree
of price stability in the postwar world requires us to meet
challenges of three sorts: the danger of purchasing-power
inflation growing out of war borrowings; the danger of an
unhealthy business boom induced by a short-lived scramble
for goods; and the final danger of a traditional postwar
collapse.

3. *Trade Barriers and Economic Nationalism*

The growth since the last war of tariff walls, import quotas,
and other impediments to world trade is a story familiar to
all. Their incidence has undoubtedly been more serious, on
the whole, in the field of finished goods than in raw materials;
but world trade in the latter has also suffered severely,
especially through the desire to create a national self-sufficiency independent of imports.

There has been a tendency to refer to trade barriers as if
they were the *enfants terribles* of the world economy—de-

stroyers of trade and prosperity out of pure mischievousness. Obviously, the explanation cannot be as simple as that. The nations of the world have not been ruining their own foreign trade from sheer perversity or ignorance. Trade barriers are the consequences of previously existing pressures. In some cases these may come from greedy domestic producers; but more often they reflect genuine difficulties at home, including unemployment, traceable to foreign underselling. There has also been the necessity of limiting imports because of a shortage of foreign exchange to pay for them; nor can the desire to diminish dependence on the outside world be considered altogether vicious in this age of global wars.

The experts of the League of Nations have recognized the relatively derived or secondary nature of trade barrier disturbances in the following words:

> To some extent it is true to say that the disequilibria in international trade were the cause of the trade barriers rather than caused by them and that to deal with the barriers alone would have meant mistaking effect for cause.[10]

Even that great economic solecism, the American tariff wall, must not be magnified beyond its true capacity for evil. Thus the London *Economist*, no friend of high duties, points out:

> Of course it may well be that the much-abused American tariff is more of an irritant than a real obstruction to the flow of trade. It is almost certainly true that any reduction in the tariff that is at all politically practicable would be wholly inadequate to solve the problem of the dollar (*i.e.*, of obtaining dollars to pay for imports from America).[11]

Our postwar plans should undoubtedly provide for intelligent and comprehensive efforts to break down the barriers to world trade. For these we have an excellent precedent in Secretary Hull's indefatigable work. We must realize that the success of such undertakings is largely tied in with our ability to promote world prosperity on other fronts. If reasonably full employment of men and resources may be attained in every land, the need for defending the home economy by tariff and quota walls will be greatly diminished. Many will argue that freer trade must come first and then full employment will follow. Whether this is true or not, we must recognize the manifold practical obstacles in the way of persuading countries to admit imports unreservedly in the *hope* of consequent exports.

The solution here, in the field of raw materials as well as processed goods, must lie in simultaneous action of several sorts. If we can set up effective international mechanisms to encourage a balanced expansion of world production, and to prevent recurrent speculative upsurges and price collapses, then at the same time we can deal more successfully with the problem of freely distributing this expanded production among all the nations of the world.

4. *Raw Materials Planning and Other Planning*

It goes without saying that the economic problems of the postwar world will not be confined to raw materials; the solutions needed must extend to other spheres, *e.g.*, over-all fiscal policy, financial reconstruction, public works, development of backward areas, general reduction of trade barriers, etc. Whatever measures are suggested for raw materials must be viewed, therefore, in their relation to a wider program. But effective treatment requires that our attention be concentrated here as closely as possible upon the raw-commodities section of the postwar economy. The reader must not assume that we underestimate the importance of other questions, or that the solutions we develop are in any sense antagonistic to plans proposed in other directions.

Chapter II

THE ISSUE OF CARTELS VERSUS
FREE PRODUCTION

"We know from experience what government cartels mean. They are worse if possible, than private cartels."

—SENATOR J. C. O'MAHONEY.[1]

"The answer to each and every problem, if the high opportunity of this and the succeeding generation is to be seized, is collaboration with the United States, not to restrict trade but to free it; not to stake out vested claims but to raise the world's share of goods and services in every place and by every means."

—*The Economist*, London, June 6, 1942, p. 782.

A T the outset of this discussion we referred to the basic dilemma arising from the seeming conflict between full production and continued stability. Based on experience, our practicable choice appears to lie between fluctuating prices together with fluctuating production—the way of free competition—and stable prices together with curtailed production—the way of the cartel.

Cartels are combinations of producers or dealers to maintain prices above a competitive level. Their continued success must depend on restricting output. They appear directly opposed in principle to the postwar ideal "of expansion of production, employment, and the exchange and consumption of goods."[2] Consequently it is easy to condemn them out of hand as sheer works of the devil operating through human greed. But if our economic choice really lies only between the two evils of unbearable fluctuations and limited output, then cartel advocates may plausibly claim that theirs is the lesser of the two misfortunes. A Harvard University apologist for cartels has expressed this viewpoint in the following energetic language:

A system of industrial organization which tends to stabilize production and to introduce changes gradually and carefully may conceivably hold

13

out greater promise of building a world without economic conflicts than the system of uncontrolled "progress" from which the world has thus far suffered. If a certain degree of rigidity is thus introduced into our economic system, we may well inquire whether this is not to be preferred over a system subject to hectic fluctuations, with recurrent loss of invested capital, unemployment and social upheaval. Even if it should prove true that cartels tend to hold back progress, this may therefore turn out to be one of the most desirable features of the cartels in a world in which not expansion but coordination of existing capacity may prove to be the greatest immediate need.[3]

Before this argument is rejected as a merely casuistical justification of selfishness it might be well to consider the hold that the cartel idea has taken upon the economic world. This is not a matter solely of agreements by big business firms seeking the advantages of monopolies. Small business has been equally cartel-minded, when practicable means—such as "fair price" laws governing retailers[4]—have been devised to this end. Interestingly enough, it is the large firms in the merchandising field that have consistently opposed such measures to limit the workings of competition. The almost forgotten National Recovery Administration was a joint adventure in cartel practice by the government and the manufacturers of the United States. Its failure can hardly be ascribed to any conscientious rejection of the principles of price fixing and limited output, but rather to the inherent weaknesses of the cartel technique, namely, the mutual mistrust of competitors and their unwillingness to submit to controls and discipline. Finally, the Agricultural Adjustment Administration can fairly be described as a governmental plan for the cartelization of the American farmer,[5] and one which has gained his effective though sometimes grudging support.

In international affairs the cartel idea has made great headway. Judged by the public's reaction there would seem to be two diametrically different types of world cartels— those set up by large corporations, which are unpatriotic and vicious, and those sponsored by governments, which are advantageous and desirable. In the first group belong the arrangements relating to synthetic rubber and oil patents, to high-speed steels, to optical glass, to industrial diamonds, to various chemicals, and to other *industrial* products. In the second group belong the agreements covering sugar, coffee, wheat, tin, tea, and sundry other *natural* products.

There are obvious grounds for distinguishing between these two types of cartel action. The corporate moves are addressed solely to private interest, and are calculated chiefly to preserve an already satisfactory profit position. The governmental agreements are entered into, for the most part, to correct disastrous price declines resulting from oversupply, and to protect the consumers' interests.[6] It must be recognized that both good and bad cartels alike reflect an underlying drift in the direction of concerted restrictions on output. Since neither private producers nor governments can possibly favor low supply for its own sake, it is clear that cartels as a whole are the world's makeshift substitute for its inability to adjust its business structure to abundance.

The government-sponsored cartels referred to above have all related to basic raw materials. It is not difficult to understand why the government has intervened on behalf of producers in this field, although it has been either neutral or actively hostile toward similar activities by manufacturers. As compared with the latter, raw-materials producers are much more numerous, less able to cartelize themselves, and subject to more violent and devastating price declines. Our American ideals of free competition, and the logic of our statutes and court decisions, have simply been outweighed and overthrown by the tragic plight of our farmers in the great depression.

When we approach the cartel question currently, and on the international level, we are confronted by a deep cleavage of opinion. In the field of raw materials the cartel has an entrenched position by virtue of the various International Commodity Agreements concluded and in prospect. Nevertheless, the desirability of arrangements of this sort has been strongly challenged in official quarters, both here and abroad.

As applied to manufactured goods the cartel system appears to be definitely unpopular in this country, but favorably regarded by the typical British industrialist.

In England there is a flourishing movement, known as the World Trade Alliance Association, headed by Sir Edgar Jones, which has as its program, "to regulate the distribution of an agreed quantity of export of each main product of every country at a stable agreed world economic price."[7] This philosophy has been vigorously attacked by British liberal journals,[8] but it remains the dominant aim among businessmen. On the other hand, the officially expressed attitude of American business organizations is directly opposed to cartels and monopolies.[9] The American conviction was emphatically expressed by Eric Johnston, president of the United States Chamber of Commerce, in speeches made by him in England in 1943.[10]

The present policy of the American government toward international cartels embracing finished goods has been variously construed. Vice-President Wallace has repeatedly attacked cartels "of the German type" as an insidious menace to the prosperity of the postwar world. The Department of Justice has been active in its prosecution of American firms having such cartel agreements with foreign manufacturers as affect our domestic market.[11] It is clear that our foreign policy would prefer to dispense completely with finished-goods cartels. Yet there are signs that we are prepared to consider the alternative of accepting them and attempting to regulate them.[12] Numerous hints have been dropped about a sensational possibility, which is nothing less than the formation of an International Board to control the raw materials of the earth. This agency is described by its supporters as a "protector of American interests against uncontrolled cartels and other combinations," in other words, as a "good cartel" to defeat the bad ones. One detailed account of the proposal states that the following questions would be subject to the decisions of the International Board:

How much of each raw material would be produced by each government and each operator;

What their prices would be if it appeared necessary to stabilize markets and production levels; and

What producers would have which markets.[13]

How seriously such a scheme is being considered by those in governmental authority, it is impossible to state. The public notice given to this type of answer to the problem of raw materials is a striking demonstration of the acute and baffling nature of the issue. Surely such a "solution" is a confession of defeat. For how can we really hope to gain abundance through restriction, and freedom through regimentation?

There is a converse conclusion to be drawn. If cartels can be avoided, or held down to a minimum role, in the field of basic commodities, it should be a much easier task to dispense with them in other sectors of the economy. This is true because the issue of cartels versus free production presents its most complex and difficult aspects at the raw-materials level, for the very reason that here alone governments tend to favor rather than to oppose them.

Buffer Stocks in Place of Cartels

In basic commodities the working alternative to the cartel principle is the stockpile principle. This issue was made quite clear in the proceedings of the United Nations Conference on Food and Agriculture, held at Hot Springs, Va., in May–June, 1943. That gathering concerned itself with agricultural commodities only, but the substance of its arguments and decisions applies equally well to industrial raw materials.

It is worth while reproducing several paragraphs from the Report of Section III of the Conference (relating to Facilitation and Improvement of Distribution), which express a basic difference of approach to the attainment of stabilized expansion.

Some delegates envisaged future arrangements chiefly in the field of the establishment and operation of buffer stocks, managed with a view, not to maintaining fixed prices, but rather to eliminating perverse fluctuations from the long-term trend. Resort should be had to quantitative controls only in exceptional cases after all other expedients had been tried. They conceded that, theoretically, quantitative controls could be operated in such a way as to adjust supply to demand with due consideration for the needs of expansion of consumption. It was their belief, however, that in practice the bodies administering them had in the past too often shown an inherent tendency to keep production at a low level in order to insure high prices.

The delegates voicing these views maintained, moreover, that for short-term fluctuations such quantitative agreements were unnecessary, as these very temporary maladjustments could be adequately met by the device of buffer stocks. It was further stressed that in the case of actual or threatening general depression as described above, quantitative control would, by its nature, have to cut down production to correspond with decreasing consumption. Such action could only cause further contraction. The desirable policy would be for some stabilizing body to continue purchases, in order to combat the deflationary tendencies.

Finally, in order to cope with the third type of disequilibrium (a more or less permanent gap between supply and demand, an eventuality which was considered to be exceptional) it may be necessary to institute quantitative control for a time. Even in such cases, however, they consider this expedient to be dangerous because in their view it tends to perpetuate the *status quo*.

Even when quantitative control could be accepted, it should be subject to stringent rules, designed to guard against restrictionist tendencies and to hasten the process of adjustment to the new conditions.

Another group of delegates, although not denying that in the past quantitative controls had sometimes shown a restrictive tendency, emphasized that such controls had always been instituted near the bottom of depressions when the position of the cooperating producing countries had already become desperate. They maintained that controls for agricultural commodities that are subject to serious cyclical influences should be established at a time when the situation is favorable and when excessive stocks have not yet made a policy of temporary contraction imperative. According to this view it is quite possible for an expansionist policy to be pursued within the framework of regulation, which can be so devised as to increase consumption. They agree that new arrangements for quantitative control will have to provide for adequate consumer representation, which will materially assist in eliminating any tendency toward unnecessary contraction.

It was upheld that the controls established in more recent years had, on the whole, served their purpose not too unsatisfactorily in that they brought about relative stability of prices and helped to dispose of oppressive world stocks, at the same time maintaining adquate supplies. These delegates were not opposed to the device of buffer stocks as such, but they believed that the operation of such pools without the backing of control arrangements would not prevent the disastrous situations to which agricultural countries have been subjected periodically. The fact that all nations in the future will be attempting to raise the level of consumption will not rule out the recurrence of serious cyclical disruptions.[14]

These opposing views were quite deftly dovetailed into Resolution XXV adopted by the conference, which reads as follows:

XXV. INTERNATIONAL COMMODITY ARRANGEMENTS

WHEREAS:

1. Excessive short-term movements in the prices of food and agricultural commodities are an obstacle to the orderly conduct of their production and distribution;

2. Extreme fluctuations of the prices of food and agricultural products aggravate general deflationary and inflationary tendencies, which are injurious to producers and consumers alike;

3. The mitigation of these influences would promote the objectives of an expansionist policy;

4. Changes in the scale and character of production to meet more effectively the world's need for food and agricultural products may in certain instances require a period of transition and international cooperation to aid producers in making necessary readjustments in their productive organization;

5. International commodity arrangements may play a useful part in the advancement of these ends but further study is necessary to establish the precise forms which these arrangements should take and whether and to what extent regulation of production may be needed;

The United Nations Conference on Food and Agriculture

RECOMMENDS:

1. That international commodity arrangements should be designed so as to promote the expansion of an orderly world economy;

2. That, to this end, a body of broad principles should, through further international discussion, be agreed upon regarding the formulation, the provisions, and the administration of such international commodity

arrangements as may be deemed feasible and desirable and should include assurance that:

   a. Such arrangements will include effective representation of consumers as well as producers;

   b. Increasing opportunities will be afforded for supplying consumption needs from the most efficient sources of production at prices fair to both consumers and producers and with due regard to such transitional adjustments in production as may be required to prevent serious economic and social dislocations;

   c. Adequate reserves will be maintained to meet all consumption needs;

   d. Provision will be made, when applicable, for the orderly disposal of surpluses;

   3. That an international organization should be created at an early date to study the feasibility and desirability of such arrangements with reference to individual commodities and, in appropriate cases, to initiate or review such arrangements to be entered into between governments, and to guide and coordinate the operations of such arrangements in accordance with agreed principles, maintaining close relations with such programs as may be undertaken in other fields of international economic activity to the end that the objective of raising consumption levels of all peoples may be most effectively served.

Behind the diplomatic language of the resolution, one may discern a deeply felt disagreement. One group clearly mistrusts international commodity arrangements as almost certain to contain the restrictionist evil of cartels. This group plumped for buffer stocks as an adequate and unobjectionable device for removing excessive short-term fluctuations in prices. The other group, contrariwise, has small faith in the stabilizing influence of stockpiles without control arrangements and believes that such agreements can be drawn in such a way as to avoid "unnecessary contraction."[15]

"Unnecessary" is the key word here. The best that can be said for carefully devised international commodity agreements is that they will hold down their restrictive effect to a practicable minimum. But this minimum is itself a highly indefinite and controversial concept. Hence considerable a priori skepticism may be justified as to the likelihood that such agreements will work out in practice "so as to promote the expansion of an orderly world economy."

Buffer-stock operations are unquestionably expansionist in their direct effects. They encourage production. But by doing so, will they not bring about the "oppressive world stocks" to which the control advocates point with alarm? To resolve this problem, the advantages and limitations of the stockpile technique must be subjected to more than superficial scrutiny.

SUMMARY

The issue of cartels versus free production is more complicated than the denouncers of cartels are generally willing to admit. Cartels have spread and will spread as long as the world lacks an effective mechanism by which balanced expansion may be achieved without a resulting disruption of prices. Government-sponsored restriction schemes for raw materials may be free from the grosser abuses found in private cartels, but the *raison d'être* of both is the same, *viz.*, to prevent abundance from damaging the price structure. The stockpile principle offers itself as a theoretically preferable alternative to curtailment of output; but it has problems of its own which must be considered with care.

Chapter III

THE PARADOX OF THE STOCKPILE

"Let no one feel that precious surpluses will bear down upon us and engulf us. . . . These are assets of tremendous value."
—BERNARD M. BARUCH and JOHN HANCOCK Report on War and Post-war Adjustment Policies, Feb. 15, 1934, p. 30.
". . . Unneeded stocks of raw materials, beyond the margin of military safety, will hang over the postwar market, depressing future production, employment, and prices. It will be stockpiling trouble for the future."
—Same report, p. 72.

THE two statements at the head of this chapter are taken from one of our most authoritative documents on post-war planning. They mirror faithfully the ambivalent attitude of practical men toward surpluses and stockpiles. It is true that, as the report says on still a third page[1] "these surpluses, properly utilized, represents tremendous wealth to ourselves and others." It is true, as Herbert Feis pointed out, that having made only trivial appropriations for stockpiles up to the fall of France, we found that "the consequences have been costly."[2] But it is equally true, as Dr. H. G. Moulton stated only six months later, that businessmen are already showing "concern over the increasing size of the so-called stockpiles."[3]

In fact the clock has already come full circle and brought us the suggestion that our wool surplus be actually *destroyed*.[4] When we reflect that this desperate idea was advanced while tailors were still prohibited from making two-trouser suits, our lack of a rational and national stockpile philosophy must be painfully manifest. This lack has in turn a vital bearing on the world's failure to achieve a balanced and expanding economy.

The obvious and simple formula for continued high-level employment is, first, to produce intelligently and on a full scale; second, to distribute as much of this production as possible by aggressive and economical means; and, finally, to store up any undistributed surplus of goods for future consumption. The third step appears to offer exasperating difficulties. The modern world is not geared properly to the storage of goods. This is the sad truth, even though on the one hand we have developed techniques of physical storage far superior to those of the past; and on the other hand, our very productivity has created a greater need than ever before for the use of commodity reservoirs or stockpiles as stabilizing mechanisms.

When we view our economic processes mainly in their physical terms—as notably under the stress of war—we recognize the stockpile as a basic necessity, similar to natural resources or productive plants. Generally speaking, the larger the supply of practically everything, the better it is for us. The exceptions are unimportant in the over-all picture, particularly since in wartime the oversupply of one year is apt to come in very handy the next.[5] We consider ourselves as strangely shortsighted in not having imported billions of dollars' worth of rubber, tin, silk, and coffee, instead of the world's gold. Even in domestic goods shortage has plagued us on all sides, despite our feverish production. Certainly we could have used to great advantage an abundant and assorted stock of raw materials and staple manufactures, both home produced and imported.

War stockpiles prepared in peacetime are not only aids to victory and guarantees against distress; they constitute also an important means of stimulating and maintaining production and employment. If we knew we were destined to enter a Third World War a quarter century from now, we should probably agree readily upon a long-term stockpile policy, looking to the accumulation of an enormous arsenal of military and civilian goods, and contributing almost as importantly to the full employment of our resources and man power. Perhaps we could then emulate Hitler who solved Germany's unemployment problem simply by preparing to conquer the world.

It seems, however, that we emerge from wars convinced that they will not occur again. Hence, hitherto we have been unwilling to create large stockpiles in peacetime as part of our long-range *military* policy. (After the First World War, in quite the contrary fashion, the armed forces disposed promptly of their vast and varied holdings of commodities.) Thus the obvious lesson of our present discomfiting shortages —which repeat faithfully the experience of the last war[6]— does not seem likely in itself to lead us to adopt comprehensive storage plans for both security and economic stability.

Why has not the stockpile principle emerged as a fundamental factor in economic policy—both national and international? Why has it failed to entrench itself in the thinking of either the man in the street or the trained economist? Why has it played so small a part to date in the literature of postwar planning?

The obvious answer is either that the stockpile principle has basic practical defects or that for some special reason it has failed to gain the appreciation it deserves. At this point an inquiry into both of these suggestions appears to be in order. In this discussion the words "stockpile" and "stockpiling" will ordinarily refer to comprehensive storage operations, under government auspices.

The claimed advantages of the stockpile idea are of two kinds: first, as a store of goods for future needs; second, as a stabilizing mechanism. No one can seriously call into question the usefulness of stockpiles on the first count. In fact, the storage device is so integral a part of our ordinary economic life that few people realize its pervasiveness. At every point in the process of production, distribution, and consumption a certain inventory or store of goods is recognized as essential to the carrying on of business. It is true— and, of course, highly significant—that modern business technique strongly favors holding down such inventories to the lowest practicable figure. Nevertheless, the aggregate of the country's industrial and commercial inventories is always an impressive percentage of a year's production or consumption of final goods—probably not less than 80 per cent.[7] To this must be added a sizable component for consumers' inventories of goods owned but held for later needs.

Storage for future use manifests itself in important ways outside the business field. Water storage is certainly the most impressive of these because (1) it is so essential to our very life; (2) it has the four separate uses of daily water supply, irrigation, flood control, and generation of power; and (3) there is never any question of having *too much* water in storage. Storage of gold as a monetary reserve has an entirely different set of uses, of which possible future need was formerly by far the most important. Stockpiling of war materials has been accepted as unquestioningly as water storage; the only issue has been as to quantity. Finally, the policy of government storage of food and other articles for civilian consumption has been followed throughout history.[8] In recent centuries the trend has indeed been away from this device. Yet the resumption of its use by Switzerland[9] as recently as 1929 indicates the vitality of the conception even under modern nonemergency conditions.

During the present war a new line of thought has developed with respect to American stockpiling of raw materials. This is based upon the rapid depletion of our national resources of many basic products and the great desirability of conserving what we have left by bringing in substantial quantities from abroad. The most energetic proponent of this viewpoint has been William L. Batt, vice chairman of the War Production Board and United States representative on the Combined Raw Materials Board and Combined Production and Resources Board. In a number of speeches[10] Mr. Batt has pointed out that our resources of iron ore, zinc, bauxite, petroleum, timber, and other vital products are "approaching an end." He suggests, therefore, that the government import and stockpile huge quantities of these materials and that these holdings be kept off the commercial markets by earmarking them for use only in a national emergency. In other words, they are to be set aside and guarded as "weapons of national security."

Mr. Batt emphasizes the fact that such imports will give us a double advantage. Not only will they supply us with an enormously valuable national reserve, but they will also make it possible for us to export correspondingly large quantities of our manufactured goods. By accepting and storing these raw materials, we shall provide the exporting countries with the funds with which to pay for their imports from us—a problem which otherwise might admit of no really satisfactory solution. It is interesting to note several intimations in our press that a deal of this kind is actually being arranged with Russia, and that Russia might annually pay for some 750 million dollars' worth of our machinery, etc., by sending us such items as nickel, chrome, and manganese for our national stockpiles.[11]

Storage of materials is thus seen to be universally necessary and advantageous in many ways. Why then should there be any limit to its use; why should it not be employed with the utmost freedom to meet the problem of temporary or even secular excess of output over consumption? A simple answer would stress the expense involved. It would not take much analysis to demonstrate that storage costs are of a small order of magnitude compared with the losses occasioned by the threefold results of excess supply, *viz.*, price collapse, curtailed production, and reduced employment. Furthermore, the value of large commodity holdings in great emergencies is beyond money calculation.

The more serious and ingrained doubts aroused by proposals for an unlimited extension of the storage principle are related to the stabilization phase of the subject. To this we must now turn our attention. The subject is a somewhat tricky one, since it is easy to argue at the outset that storage is either a stabilizing or an unstabilizing economic device. If goods pressed for sale during a period of oversupply are bought for storage, the immediate effect is clearly toward stability, since otherwise the price would break with additional disturbing consequences. The longer term effect could conceivably be unsettling and unsound. The stored goods might be regarded as an actual or a potential addition to the market supply and thus exert a continuously depressing effect on prices; or else the maintenance of the individual price level at a time of overproduction might prevent the desirable economic effects of a lower price, *viz.*, reduced production and increased consumption of the overabundant article, and a transfer of capital and labor to other fields.

The latter objections have here been stated in the somewhat theoretical terms in which the economists tend to urge them. The businessman also has an underlying mistrust of large stocks of commodities based upon his practical experience. He knows that periods of prosperity are marked by growing inventories and that this factor in turn is always found to have been an element of weakness in the business picture and a prime cause of subsequent depression. Furthermore, the liquidation of his own excessive inventories has frequently been responsible for his major losses in unprofitable years.

The acquisition of large commodity inventories for commercial purposes *by governments* has generally resulted in financial loss to them. The most striking operation of this kind in recent times was the purchase of huge amounts of wheat and cotton by the Federal Farm Board, beginning in 1930. Because of the heavy cost of this venture (300 million dollars), the Roosevelt agricultural policy has insisted upon tying in its crop loans or purchases with a definite program of acreage curtailment. Thus the famous Ever-normal Granary proposal of Wallace received legislative sanction only as an incidental part of an elaborate scheme for crop control.[12]

During this war the government has been accumulating huge stockpiles to meet military demands. A report of the operations of the Reconstruction Finance Corporation up to Mar. 7, 1943, listed loans and commitments of over 3.7 billion dollars for the acquisition of 22 specified commodities.[13] The greater part of this huge sum must have represented stockpiles on hand. As the war progressed, certain of these stocks grew larger than foreseeable needs. The authorities were thus confronted with problems closely resembling the old bugbear of surplus.

Perhaps the first embarrassment developed in relation to wool. At the beginning of 1944 about 320 million pounds of foreign and 220 million pounds of domestic wool were held by two government agencies. Since these quantities were larger than required and since there were commitments to acquire further production both at home and abroad, the owning agencies took steps to sell certain amounts in the open market. This brought sharp complaints from both domestic producers and users. As already noted, one producer went so far as to propose a Boston Tea Party to abolish the surplus. Thus even in the midst of war's privations the specter of overabundance already shows itself, and that last insanity of human minds—destruction of the earth's bounty to bolster prices—is again astir.[14]

In the meantime similar surpluses of various metals began to accumulate, and mining men expressed similar apprehension as to their commercial position, not only at the war's end but even earlier. It is clear from various discussions in the press that the lead, zinc, and copper producers are skeptical of the actual workings of any government stockpile plan. They fear that even though they are earmarked to meet a national emergency they may be "dumped" on the market by some economy-minded administration.[15]

These anxieties are reflected in the quotation from Dr. Moulton's address referred to early in this chapter. Yet so contradictory are the various aspects of this subject that at the very same time economists were talking about exactly the opposite danger. This appears from the following item, published toward the end of 1943:

Postwar raw materials control on an international scale is coming in for increasing discussion. Fears are generally expressed that in a scramble for supplies on the international market, prices could be bid up to inflationary levels. One plan being discussed is to set up government monopolies for the purchase of raw materials in cooperation with other governments.[16]

The *London Times* even questioned the advisability of W. L. Batt's proposal for establishing noncommercial emergency reserves of strategic commodities on the ground that in the early postwar years demand for many materials "will exceed the maximum supplies from current production." Hence it sees a danger that Batt's stockpile would create a series of artificial shortages with the concomitant of artificially high prices.[17]

So far this discussion of stockpile theory and practice must appear exceedingly confusing. On the one hand, such reserves are praised as necessary, advantageous, and in universal use; on the other hand, they are viewed with suspicion as the cause of heavy loss to business and government. These diametrically opposed attitudes are projecting themselves into our current thinking on postwar surpluses. Here is the paradox to which our chapter heading refers.

This confusion may be resolved if we perceive and hold fast to a basic distinction, which provides the touchstone by which sound stockpile procedure may be identified. Whether a commodity reserve system will function as a national asset or as a national liability depends upon the mechanism under which it operates. *It is entirely a question of technique.* A stockpile is beneficial and nonembarrassing if it is set up *solely to meet future needs.* When the objective is primarily that of *early sale*, then a stockpile is likely to prove unsettling to the markets and expensive to those who hold it.

This distinction applies even in the field of private commerce, but it is by no means identical with the radical's contrast between production for use and production for profit. Those inventories which may be considered as an integral part of the mechanism of production and distribution need not constitute a vulnerable sector of the commercial economy; they are similar in their function to the plant account and the receivables which make up the businessman's productive capital. It is inventory holdings that are purchased primarily for speculative profit—and particularly those financed by larger than average bank loans—that have created financial troubles recurrently and have brought inventories as a whole into a certain kind of disrepute.[18]

Even a very large inventory measured in dollars need not constitute a special hazard to a business enterprise if the holding is normal for the type of industry. This is well illustrated by the cigarette companies, which are accustomed to carry a three years' supply of tobacco in cure, by the liquor concerns with their large stocks of aging whiskies, and the general practice in the lumber industry.[18] This practice could not be common in industry generally, even if the hazard of inventory fluctuations were removed by special accounting devices. For such devices would require an initial markdown of the capital values on the books, and furthermore the purchase of unnecessarily large inventories would entail the tying up of funds in nonprofitable holdings.

We can see, therefore, that on the one hand there need be no inherent economic weakness in the principle of stockpiling to create an abundance of goods for future use. On the other hand, such accumulation is not well suited to the bookkeeping techniques of modern business, even though in ancient times it may have been a natural and salutary byproduct of the accumulation of individual wealth.[19] It follows, therefore, that broad-gauged stockpiling policy must now become the function of the government—to meet the challenges of peace as well as to meet the exigencies of war. It is vitally necessary that the government's reserves of commodities be so operated as to constitute neither a continuing threat to the commercial markets nor a continuing focus of political pressure from interested groups.

Government stockpiling emerges as an inherently logical means both for creating desirable commodity reserves and for interposing a stabilizing buffer between supply and demand. It is one of several powerful weapons of economic control which have been forged on the anvil of the world's experience during the past 30 years. Other weapons with which it may be compared include public works programs, budgetary policy (deficit spending, etc.), credit controls, government loans to business and homeowners, and monetary changes. The stockpile device is by no means the only one needed to promote full production and employment. Nor can it necessarily be applied throughout the full range of our economic process with equal success at every point.

The reservoir principle would appear far more effective in the field of the comparatively few major raw materials than in the multiplicity of finished goods. The technical problems are all much simpler when dealing with the storable staple commodities. If stabilization can be effected as regards these key items, it is certain to have a powerful stabilizing effect upon the balance of the economy. For the great disturbances in general business are largely tied in with wide fluctuations in the price level for raw materials. In addition, a stockpile of raw materials will make possible the speedy creation of such finished goods as may be required in any emergency or as may be advantageously employed to improve our standard of living.

If we concentrate our attention on world economic policy we find that there the stockpile idea has an especial practicality. Raw-materials problems are international problems; they call for international solutions. Stockpiling can be carried out on a world scale without requiring either a world supergovernment or elaborate and closely knit economic cooperation among nations. While most other politico-economic devices can more readily be adopted on a national than an international scale, the commodity reservoir principle lends itself with relative ease to world application and its effectiveness gains particularly from that wider scope.

We have already made it clear that buffer stocks, or commodity reserves, will occupy the foremost place in our proposed plans for raw materials. In the next chapter our attention will be concentrated on the techniques actually employed to date in dealing with commodity surpluses. This is intended to show the inherent deficiencies of measures which reject or slight the stockpile principle and to lay the foundation for the concrete proposal which is to follow.

Chapter IV

FORMER SOLUTIONS FOR THE RAW MATERIALS PROBLEM

"The only effective alternatives appear to be fairly unrestricted competition with its attendant evils, or complete and individual dictation to millions of producers, with its attendant evils."
—R. F. MARTIN, "International Raw Commodity Price Control," The Brookings Institution, 1937, p. 14.

IT is sometimes said that we cannot talk intelligently about the postwar economic world unless we have definite ideas as to the structure of the postwar political world. Whether the United Nations are welded into a political entity, whether there are to be regional confederations, or whether there is to be merely a new League of Nations with greater power are matters to be decided before drawing economic blueprints. The course of our thinking need not be so circumscribed as that. A number of economic plans can readily be developed that will be valid in any future political setup except one of near anarchy. In general the simplest method is to assume a political world consisting of individual countries, such as we have today. Whatever plans are found feasible for such a world will be even more readily effective in a closer grouping of the nations.

In like measure the drawing of plans on an international scale need not be affected greatly by assumptions as to the political "climate" in individual countries. Governments as widely different as the British and the Russian expect to carry on close relationships in peace as in war. Such international agencies as affect exchange rates, general foreign trade, or raw materials will be concerned but little with the domestic politics or political economies of the participating nations. Consequently we need not be detained in our discussion by alternative hypotheses as to the spread of conservatism, liberalism, or communism. Our attention may be concentrated almost exclusively on the economic side of the problem; the political question will enter with respect more to local expediency than to world-wide political organization.

In considering plans for the future it is natural to inquire first what measures have already been tried and what was their success. In the field of raw materials we can distinguish four broad types of policy, of which one has been worked out on the international and three on the national scale. These may be identified as follows:

1. *International Commodity Agreements.* The basic factor is allocation of marketing quotas to producing nations. Other elements have included import quotas; control of production; prohibition against expanding acreage, exporting seeds, etc.; and buffer stocks.

2. *U.S. Agricultural Adjustment Administration (AAA).* The basic elements here are control of acreage and marketing quotas. Inducements to farmers include bonus payments and crop loans. The latter, in turn, create the ever-normal granary feature.

3. *Brazilian Coffee Control Scheme.* The spectacular element here has been the continued burning of huge amounts of coffee in order to bring supply into balance with demand. The planting of new trees was prohibited except for replacement.

4. *Federal Farm Board* (1930–1933). This was stabilization by government purchase only.

Of these four approaches to stabilization it seems evident that the most serious attention should be paid to the International Commodity Agreements, since they are even now in operation and are the only measures that have enlisted multinational support. Similarly, the least impressive would seem to be our Farm Board technique, which was liquidated at a huge loss in 1933 and apparently has not been attempted since in any country.

1. *International Commodity Agreements*

Beyond doubt these agreements will play an important part in the postwar economy. Even in the midst of the war

(June, 1942) a preliminary accord was reached with respect to wheat, which will be submitted to all interested countries as soon as conditions permit. A similar type of agreement governing coffee was adopted—also during wartime (1940)—by 14 producing nations and by the United States as the chief consumer. Sugar agreements have been in operation in most years since 1931 and will certainly be reestablished after the war.

In the case of all three commodities the most recent agreements represent an important advance over the old-style arrangements, which were entered into solely by the producers concerned. The new technique calls for participation by importing nations to assure adequate protection of consumer interests. One method of doing this, as provided in the wheat agreement, is by setting up minimum world stocks to guard against shortages and consequent high prices.[1]

With these improvements in prospect, may we conclude that the International Commodity Agreements will constitute in themselves an adequate and satisfactory machinery for stabilizing the position of world raw materials? On this point there is room for rather serious doubts. The general theory of the new-type agreement seems quite unobjectionable; both producer and consumer are represented and protected, and an adequate but nonexcessive supply is guaranteed. Still the practical outcome of this, as any other scheme, is likely to be found in the matter of *emphasis*. The driving force behind these agreements comes from the producing countries. Their keener financial interest in the subject is likely to give them a dominant voice in the specific arrangements. This human factor, constantly at work, will in the end create stronger provisions on the side of curtailed production and high prices than in the direction of plentiful and cheap supplies.

The more subtle dangers inherent in the International Commodity Agreement technique have been pointed out skillfully by J. S. Davis in several studies, *e.g.*, his analysis of the 1942 wheat agreement, published by the *Food Research*

Institute, and his two papers entitled "International Commodity Agreements in the Postwar World."[2] The present writer is in substantial agreement with Dr. Davis's analysis and with his highly cautious endorsement of the Commodity Agreement approach.

The acid test of the underlying soundness of the Commodity Agreements may perhaps be found in the price policy that animates them. The effect of these agreements should, of course, be helpful to the product's price, in the sense that demoralized markets and completely unremunerative returns are prevented. The technique of curtailment should not be carried so far as to create a price level for the commodity relatively *higher* than that of nonagreement commodities. When this happens, the camel has come much too far into the tent. The emphasis has passed from emergency rescue work, or first-aid assistance, to creating a special-privilege, cartelistic position for the subject commodity.

It should be laid down as a principle of operation, and as a condition for enlisting the support of the consuming nations, that curtailment schemes shall not be utilized to push the price of any commodity up to its full "parity" and certainly not beyond such parity. For this purpose we may take as our "parity" base the last 10-year average price of the particular commodity as against raw materials generally. It is important to insist on so moderate a price policy; otherwise, there is almost certain to be a strong tendency for the moving spirits behind a Commodity Agreement—*i.e.*, the producers' associations—to use the powerful machinery set up therein for the realization of a "satisfactory price." This innocent sounding objective is likely to mean a level, as J. S. Davis warns, "typically well above economic normals."

On this point the views of the League of Nation's delegates, in 1939, as summed up by Dennery, are of considerable interest:

Furthermore, price stabilization, when achieved, is always a stabilization upward. If the consumer is assured stability he will consent perhaps willingly to pay for it by a slight advance in price. But, as Rowe says, "when the president of one of the largest tin companies of Malaysia tells him that the Orient could produce with profit all the tin the world needs at a price of £70 per ton, when he must pay £230, it is not surprising that the industrialist and other tin consumers consider that the price paid for stability is too high, and the restriction scheme for tin is nothing other than a greedy monopoly." In fact, several of these plans have permitted producers to realize, thanks to high prices imposed on consumers, profits sometimes quite impressive. The Chilean nitrate monopoly obtained for the Chilean companies, from 1920 to 1927, dividends ranging from 25 to 50 per cent; the tin and rubber restriction schemes permitted, at the beginning at least, a rapid increase in the profit of these enterprises.[3]

An indication of the more recent attitude of the commodity cartel interests on the matter of price and production policies may be found in the following dispatch from London to *The Wall Street Journal*:

Those who believe that by restricting production we may solve our economic problems give up slowly. Though the International Tea Committee pays lip service to the Hot Springs dogmas, acknowledging that "the real remedy for excessive supplies is expansion of markets," it still thinks in terms of restriction of output. This is reflected in its estimate that excess world productive capacity in the postwar period will be 215 million pounds. But it is making no suggestion that lower prices will be a means to stimulate consumption.

If the restrictive spirit is to be exercised by postwar drafters of international agreements on such items as tea, wheat, tin, and rubber, they will all have to think again.[4]

Against the view of the International Tea Committee may be set the more judicious and statesmanlike utterance of the Federation of British Industries:

Extension of international commodity agreements may be desirable, but that is not the complete solution. We must envisage a future in which there will be an expanding world economy, and for this a positive not a negative policy is needed.[5]

To summarize: International Commodity Agreements will undoubtedly play a large part in the world's efforts to promote price stability in raw materials. Nevertheless, they represent a second-best type of solution, in somewhat the same way as do tariffs, ship subsidies, and all the other familiar protective weapons in the economic arsenal. They must, in consequence, be employed with great circumspection. Preferably they should be tied with some other approach to the stabilization question which will place *its* emphasis upon over-all expansion of production and consumption.

2. *The AAA Approach*

The AAA has been operating in this country for more than ten years. Consequently the elaborate system of production and price control which it represents must be viewed seriously as a possible pattern for world planning. However, it seems to belong more properly on the intranational level of agricultural control, rather than as a program to be adopted by international agreement. In other words, an AAA type of arrangement might well be the necessary sequel within various countries of their participation in a world agreement limiting their exports. Yet it is unlikely that such a world agreement would go so far as to prescribe the means by which the several nations would implement the scheme within their own borders and among their own producers. This should not deter us from considering what contribution the AAA technique may make to solving the problem of our own and other countries.

The AAA contains a number of different features which operate with varying degrees of satisfaction from one year to another. It thus becomes easy to build up an imposing mass of adverse criticism by concentrating on the instances in which we should or might have fared better without the AAA. Elementary fairness requires that we recognize that the program has been dealing with one of our country's most refractory problems, that a perfect solution is impossible, and that even the most intelligent arrangements might prove quite unwise in retrospect because of the unpredictable behavior of weather and wars.

The AAA is in fact a very ingenious and flexible instrument of control. It can in theory be employed equally well to encourage abundance as to enforce curtailment. By its system of local administration, as well as by its insistence on a heavy majority vote to put its quotas into effect, it has retained the direction of the farmers' affairs generally within their own hands. It created—even though somewhat against its will—a good-sized store of grain and cotton, which has proved of great advantage under the impact of war.

The really serious defect of the AAA is that it is a quasi-cartel system. It reproduces within our country the same institutional weaknesses that are inherent in the International Commodity Agreements above discussed. Even though both producers and consumers may be represented in the making of policy, the driving force of self-interest tends to put the producers in the saddle.

It can hardly be denied that the farmers have dominated the AAA and that they have exerted great and effective political pressure to make it yield them the financial returns to which they believe themselves entitled. To the farmers this course of conduct must appear entirely right and proper. Why not fight hard for justice and a fair return? But the impartial student will detect a serious catch in the logic. Of course, the farmers are entitled to fight for their rights as hard as anyone else, but they are not entitled to marshal the great powers of government to guarantee them their hearts' desire. The farmers appealed to the government for help, in the first instance, because their plight was desperate. In view of the emergency they were afforded a special type of assistance—privileges quite different from those enjoyed by businessmen engaged in other unremunerative lines. Is there not a real danger that they will ultimately have turned their misfortunes into a source of undue power? For any group which is permitted to use government to obtain for itself "*merely" the full measure of what it believes it deserves* is certain to get a great deal more, relatively, than its fellow groups.

By the nature of things the AAA technique tends toward restriction much more than toward abundance. In seeking to achieve a balance between production and consumption of the individual crops, it can find its only trustworthy instrument in curtailment of output where surplus appears a chronic evil. It has no means of promoting consumption on any large scale, nor can it afford to risk the accumulation of enormous stores of two or three commodities in the hope that somehow a huge emergency demand will develop. Thus it happens that the ever-normal granary feature of the AAA shows itself as a hesitant rather than a broad-visioned step toward abundance. In truth, the large cotton and wheat stocks that came into the government's hands in recent years were far from the result of deliberate planning; on the contrary they were thrust upon it by a combination of favorable weather and more intensive farming methods. The AAA regarded these stocks more as a headache than as an asset.

Severe critics of the AAA go farther than the above and blame its restrictive program for the fact that our food resources in 1943 were insufficient to meet war demands.[6] This is hardly fair. There appears no reason to believe that the country's stocks of wheat and corn would have been larger had we permitted all farmers to produce and sell as they pleased over the past 10 years.

Our evaluation of the AAA approach is essentially the same as that of the Commodity Agreement approach. Both are workable means of preventing ruinous prices. Both suffer from the underlying fault that they are oriented toward restriction and scarcity. Both need to be integrated with some other technique which emphasizes and encourages a balanced abundance.

3. *The Brazilian Coffee-control Approach*

It goes without saying that we are unsympathetic to any plan which necessitates destruction of a useful commodity. The experience of Brazil is mentioned only because it demonstrates with shocking clearness that a control scheme *dealing with a single commodity* must inevitably find its remedy in contraction. There was nothing Brazil could do to create a world purchasing power adequate to consume all her coffee, even though the potential demand was there without question. Brazil burned 100 billion pounds of coffee for the same basic reason as our steel industry operates in depression at less than half capacity. These measures, deplorable as they appear, are the only practicable means by which a single commodity or a single industry can adapt itself to an inadequate and highly inelastic market demand. In the case of Brazil, buying up the coffee and burning it proved a more practicable technique than reducing the coffee crop proportionately. The implication is clear that a program looking to *expansion* must deal with not one or two but a number of basic commodities.

4. *The Federal Farm Board Approach*

All those who advocate the accumulation of commodity stocks for future use must study with care the experience of our Farm Board between 1929 and 1933. This agency endeavored to support the price of wheat and cotton by large-scale purchases. When it ceased to buy, the price collapsed, and the board later sold out its holdings at a heavy loss. This record is constantly pointed to as the most spectacular of many proofs that valorization or government-purchase schemes are almost certain to fail badly, unless accompanied by a program of restriction and regimentation.

Such a conclusion is broadly correct when applied to valorization schemes as they are commonly understood, *viz.*, government purchases to support the price until the commodity may be *sold*—usually abroad—at a suitable level. The conclusion is not correct when applied to a comprehensive policy of purchasing commodities for future *use*, with the collateral object of reducing price fluctuations. This was the essential character of the Chinese Ever-normal Granary, which operated with conspicuous success in that country for many centuries.[7] It applies also to the reserves of many materials set up for war emergencies in all ages, and, in a significant degree also, to standard policies of *gold* acquisition and storage.

It is certain that the world economic program of the future will include the creation of buffer stocks of primary commodities, to offset temporary maladjustments of supply and demand and to prevent wide fluctuations in prices. This program will work badly if the buffer stocks are quasi-commercial in character and if emphasis is placed upon their quick disposal in the market. It will work well if, among other requisites, the stockpiles can function as part of the true wealth of the world and if their basic role is to anticipate, to stimulate, and to satisfy the limitless consumptive demands of the human race.

General Conclusion

None of the four approaches briefly discussed above has won our unqualified approval. World planning for raw materials needs something beyond what has gone before. The new or perfected mechanism must still be closely related to techniques which we have tried and fully understand. In the case of those crops which pose a *chronic* problem of surplus, International Commodity Agreements and domestic regulation measures appear inevitable in practice and possibly justifiable in theory. This justification must come from a synthesis of these control schemes with the wider aim of balanced abundance. In that manner, restrictive control becomes the exception—a necessary but temporary evil—which will become of steadily diminishing importance as the living standards of the world are developed. In the next chapters such a synthesis is presented in some detail.

Chapter V

A SPECIFIC PROPOSAL FOR INTERNATIONAL STABILIZATION OF RAW MATERIALS

"It is probably true to say that all the rational arguments which can be advanced in favor of the gold standard apply even more strongly to this proposal, which is at the same time free from the defects of the former."

—F. A. HAYEK, "A Commodity Reserve Currency," *The Economic Journal*, June–September, 1943, p. 184.

"For a world that is happy and at peace is a world of well-filled barns."

—CLARE LEIGHTON, "Give Us This Day," New York, 1943.

Preliminary Assumption as to Price Level

Stabilization presupposes a price level at which or around which to stabilize. No one writing in 1944 can determine in advance a suitable price level for basic commodities, whether stated in gold, in paper dollars, or in any other terms. The principles and the mechanics of our proposal are, however, independent of the price level to which they are to be applied. For the sake of clear exposition, one or more specific levels need to be assumed. Our calculations will be based alternatively on the average dollar prices of 1926, which are about the same as at the beginning of 1944, and on the averages prevailing in 1937. If a higher level than either of these proves necessary because of the length of the war, our dollar values can be readily increased in proportion. We might point out that the Beveridge Report on "Social Security for Britain" also used figures based on the current price level, subject to later adjustment.[1]

PART I. GENERAL OR COMPOSITE STABILIZATION

A. Brief Summary of the Proposal

An international agency—say, International Commodity Corporation (ICC)—will purchase, hold, and sell primary commodities on a composite or unit basis. The commodity unit will consist of 15 or more products, their relative quantities corresponding to their world production and exports. Purchases will be made whenever units are available at a composite price slightly below the stabilized value and sales will be made when the composite price advances slightly above that level.

The corporation will best operate as a subsidiary of an International Monetary Bank or Fund (IMF) from which it will obtain its capital. This bank may be the agency for stabilizing foreign exchange rates in line with the various plans—White, Keynes, etc.—now under discussion. These funds in turn will be supplied by the central banks of participating countries in the form of deposits with the IMF and may thus be considered as part of the monetary reserves of such central banks. In this way the commodity-unit holdings of ICC will function as the equivalent of world currency.

The commodities will be stored in the first instance in the country of purchase. Creditor nations of the IMF will have the right to take over and hold physical possession of an appropriate amount of commodity units, with the provision that they defray the storage expense.

B. More Detailed Explanation and Discussion

1. *The Commodity Unit.* A tentative 15-commodity unit is outlined in the appended table, which indicates also the method of derivation of the relative quantities. The relationship of the 15 commodities selected from the entire field of raw materials is developed statistically in Appendix I. Nine commodities in our list are of major rank with respect both to value of world production and value of world trade. These are wheat, corn, sugar, cotton, wool, tobacco, petroleum, coal, and wood pulp. One, pig-iron, is of first rank in world production but not in world trade. The remaining five—coffee, tea, rubber, copper, and tin—are of first rank in world trade, though not in world production. About five-eighths of the

unit is made up of agricultural products and about one-third represents food.

The number of commodities in the unit might ultimately be considerably larger—say 25 to 30. It would seem best to operate the system at the outset with a readily manageable number of products, and to expand the group gradually—

TABLE I.—ILLUSTRATIVE COMPOSITION OF A 15-COMMODITY UNIT BASED ON 1937
PRODUCTION, EXPORTS, AND PRICES
A. Data Based on World Production*

| Commodity | Production | | Average price, cents | Value of output, millions | Quantity of the commodity in $100 unit, based on production |
	Unit	Quantity, millions			
Wheat...................	bu.	3,858	112.0	4,325	15.0
Corn....................	bu.	4,592	67.0	3,077	17.7
Cotton..................	lb.	16,280	12.0	1,954	65.0
Wool....................	lb.	3,612	30.0	1,084	14.4
Rubber..................	lb.	2,550	18.5	472	10.1
Coffee..................	lb.	3,668	8.9	327	14.5
Tea.....................	lb.	1,032	22.5	232	4.0
Sugar...................	lb.	55,000	2.6	1,430	213.1
Tobacco.................	lb.	3,850	32.0	1,232	149.0
Total agricultural......	....	......	......	14,133	
Petroleum...............	bbl.	1,968	124.00	2,440	7.6
Coal....................	l. ton	1,300	404.00	5,252	5.0
Wood pulp...............	lb.	51,200	2.05	1,050	200.0
Pig iron................	l. ton	90	23.00	2,070	0.35
Copper..................	lb.	4,943	0.13	643	19.2
Tin.....................	lb.	440	53.00	233	1.71
Total nonagricultural...	....	......	......	11,688	
Grand total.............	....	......	......	25,821	

* Excluding Russia and China.

say at the rate of one commodity per year—after the plan has been well tested by experience.

2. *Purchases of the Commodity Unit.* We shall assume that world prices for the component commodities are calculated f.o.b. principal ports of shipment, in dollar equivalents. These will thus be export prices familiar to world trading operations and easily determinable. When the composite price falls to 95 per cent of the base, ICC will buy

appropriate amounts of all 15 commodities in the world export markets, including therein purchases on the commodity exchanges. The operations will be patterned as closely as possible upon the commercial purchases regularly made by importing nations. Purchases in the various primary markets should ordinarily be proportioned to the related

TABLE I.—ILLUSTRATIVE COMPOSITION OF A 15-COMMODITY UNIT BASED ON 1937 PRODUCTION, EXPORTS, AND PRICES.—(*Continued*)

B. Data Based on World Exports

Commodity	Exports		Quantity in $100 unit, based on exports	Result $100 unit based on average of production basis and export basis	
	Quantity, millions	Value, millions		Quantity	Value at 1937 price
Wheat...................	633	709	9.0	12 bu.	$ 13.40
Corn....................	514	345	7.51	12½ bu.	8.40
Cotton..................	7,423	891	108.7	87 lb.	10.50
Wool...................	2,400	720	35.1	25 lb.	7.50
Rubber..................	2,550	472	37.3	24 lb.	4.50
Coffee..................	3,668	327	53.7	34 lb.	3.00
Tea....................	989	223	14.5	9¼ lb.	2.10
Sugar...................	26,350	685	386.0	300 lb.	7.80
Tobacco.................	1,207	386	17.7	16.3 lb.	5.20
Total agricultural........	....	4,758	......	....	$ 62.40
Petroleum...............	340	422	5.0	6.3 bbl.	$ 7.80
Coal...................	123	497	1.8	3.4 l. ton	13.70
Wood pulp..............	14,200	289	208.0	204.0 lb.	4.20
Pig-iron................	7.5	113	0.11	0.23 l. ton	5.30
Copper..................	3,500	455	513.0	35.0 lb.	4.50
Tin....................	440	233	6.4	4.0 lb.	2.10
Total non-agricultural....	....	2,069	......	....	$ 37.60
Grand total.............	....	6,827	......	....	100.00

production or possibly exports, contingent, however, on storage arrangements discussed in the next section. Futures contracts may be bought in place of spot-delivery commodities, whenever the former are obtainable at a discount.

3. *Storage Arrangements.* It is suggested that storage expense be distributed between producing nations, holding nations, and participants generally on some rational basis. The storage burden should fall upon the vendor nations that

will benefit most directly from the purchase operations. Perhaps each nation should agree to provide free storage of commodities sold by it to ICC, for a period of not more than two years. This storage burden may in turn be assumed by the producers or even the commodity exchanges, subject to government supervision.[2] If the commodity is provisionally stored in the interior, the producing country must complete delivery to the port of shipment when requested.

Nations holding deposits with the IMF, who thus have helped finance the purchase of units, should have the privilege of holding up to an equivalent amount of units in their own custody. This they may wish to do for their general protection. In such case they must pay delivery costs from the nearest available port of shipment and assume the cost of storage thereafter. They will then hold the units as agents for ICC, and will have the privilege of drawing out individual commodities and replacing them by future contracts whenever this is advantageous. Alternatively, creditor nations may be given the right to purchase units from ICC at 100 per cent of base value, thus cancelling an equivalent amount of their money claim.

Unit commodities still held in the producing country two years after purchase will then be stored at the expense of ICC at the most economical rate. Storage arrangements will include suitable rotation to preserve the commodities in merchantable condition.

4. *Sales of Commodity Units.* Whenever the composite price of the unit commodities advances to 105 per cent of the base, the corporation will sell out complete commodity units. This will be done as long as the market will take them at the 105 per cent level and as long as there are commodity units available for sale. Both purchase and sale policy will thus be entirely automatic; the purchasing will be unlimited as to potential quantity and the selling will be limited only by the supply on hand.

We pointed out above that "holding nations" will be free to sell out individual spot commodities whenever they can be replaced more cheaply by future contracts. The same will apply to any other commodities belonging to the corporation. The profit on such exchanges will go to the corporation.

5. *Financing Details.* The corporation will obtain its funds by sale of its notes to the IMF. The notes will bear a nominal interest rate. The IMF in turn will hold these notes as reserve assets against its liabilities, which will consist of deposits and capital stock held by the central banks of the participating nations.

The financial transactions involved in the corporation's operations will be similar to those resulting from international trade generally. The location of its headquarters, *e.g.*, whether at Geneva, London, or New York, should not affect the transfer problems. Transfers may be made in the first instance by credits and debits to the central bank account on the books of the IMF. In essence, purchases by the corporation will be equivalent to exports from the vendor nations to the financing nations. The United States will undoubtedly do a large part both of the selling and the financing. In combination, this will have the economic effect of governmental purchases from our own private producers. The storage arrangements, also, will probably result in our holding physical custody of commodity units at least equivalent to the commodities which the corporation acquires in this country.

6. *Extent of the Corporation's Operations, and Monetary Effects.* No precise calculation can be made of the amount of purchases that will be needed to maintain the composite price level at 95 per cent of normal. However, some tentative conclusions may be advanced on this point, as follows:

The published figures for world stocks of seven commodities showed a group increase of about 50 per cent from 1929 to 1932, and a return to the original levels in 1937. During the same period the price index declined about 60 per cent and then recovered about two-thirds of its loss. (These are annual average figures from the Survey of Current Business). Within this time there was no significant change in over-all production of agricultural commodities, but mineral output fluctuated widely.

Normal stocks of basic commodities seem to average about three to four months' supply.[3] It appears, therefore, that the increase in stocks associated with extreme depression, over a three-year period, was in the vicinity of 15 per cent of a year's production. Were prices to be maintained at slightly under normal, there would seem no reason to expect greatly increased production, but consumption would undoubtedly be larger than in deep depression because of higher purchasing power. Hence, one-seventh of a year's production would appear to be the maximum absorption necessary to maintain the price level over a three-year period—say, at the rate of 5 per cent per year. It seems doubtful that such purchases would have to be made for three years in succession, since the price pendulum would probably swing upward before then. We must take into account the psychological effect of the price floor, the direct economic effect of increased producers' incomes, and also the further supporting influence of stabilization programs in individual commodities, discussed below.

On the one hand, the total funds needed to operate on a 15-commodity basis may be estimated as on the order of 5 billion dollars. If the number is eventually increased, say, to 25, the funds involved may reach a maximum of 7 billion dollars. All this may be considered as an addition to the monetary supply of the world during the period of acquisition of units. On the other hand, it may be expected that a large portion of the units accumulated during periods of business recession will be drawn out into consumption when general activity expands. To that extent the commodity-unit reservoir will be self-liquidating as well as self-financing.

7. *A World Ever-normal Granary.* The commodity-unit holdings of the corporation will constitute buffer stocks and as such will meet a universally recognized need of the post-war world. During their periods of growth these stocks will interpose a buffer between world markets and surplus production threatening to demoralize the price level. Con-

versely, when demand tends to outrun supply, these stocks will be drawn upon and thus act as a buffer to prevent a drastic upswing of prices.

It seems logical to assume that the corporation's reserves will show secular growth, *i.e.*, there will be an underlying tendency for its purchases to exceed its sales. Strong arguments may be made for welcoming a steady increase in its stocks, on the ground that their value as real wealth and as emergency reserves far exceeds the offsetting factor of storage costs. To the extent that possible war may still enter into the picture the case for large stocks becomes stronger, especially from the standpoint of depositing nations such as the United States. We can hold our share of the corporation's commodity units within our own borders and view them as a war chest of enormous value.

While the nations should act in concert in the corporation's buying and selling policies, they would retain freedom of separate action in the use of the stored commodities. In addition to the right to hold stocks on behalf of the corporation, each depositing nation will, of course, have the right to purchase and take over any of the stocks, on a composite basis. The United States, for example, might elect to build up its social security reserves in the form of such commodity holdings—a logical policy, which would earmark a large store of commodities for a specific future use.[4]

It is possible to set up a standard mechanism whereby the corporation's holdings will not overpass some agreed-on maximum. After this maximum point is reached, the depositing nations will then be called upon to take over proportionate amounts of future purchases. They will also be expected to put into effect social measures for increasing the consumption of these commodities, the exact methods to be left to each to decide. The stamp plan might well be applied in the field of foods, fibers, and fuels. With respect to the metals, expanded consumption might be effected through public works programs.

The American stamp plan, which distributed surplus foods and cotton goods free to lower income groups, operated for several years with practically no serious criticism from any responsible source. It is expected to be revived even before the war ends. This invention was perhaps the most revolutionary of all the New Deal measures. These two facts deserve careful reflection. May they not mean that new economic devices are not necessarily unsound, and that the more closely and directly a plan attacks the central question of making surpluses available to those that can use them, the more likely it is to prove feasible and worth while?

Interestingly enough, British businessmen have been considering the possibility of dealing with surpluses along these lines. The Conservative party has suggested that the government might finance the bulk purchases of universally desirable household goods. Samuel Courtauld, the liberal industrialist, has gone further and suggested that in depressions the government might not only buy up such goods but also distribute them at low prices or even give them away to needy classes at home or abroad. "So long as the articles were only distributed to people who really needed them and were in fact too poor to buy them in the ordinary market, this would not undermine the demand from the normal public. On the contrary, it would, by keeping up the earnings of labor, tend to keep up the normal demand for consumption goods."[5]

We advance the further suggestion that a substantial part of the purchases made *above the point of maximum stocks* be donated by the depositing (richer) nations to other countries with lower living standards. Such philanthropy should not only bring moral satisfaction but it may also pay large dividends in the form of world peace and prosperity.

PART II. INTERNATIONAL AGREEMENTS RELATING TO
INDIVIDUAL COMMODITIES

The purchase and sale of commodity units on a composite basis will allow full play for market forces affecting the relative prices of the component items. For example, while the unit value remains at 100, it will still be possible for corn to rise from $0.80 to $1 and cotton to fall from $0.20 to $0.15 because of crop or other developments.

We are convinced that a substantial degree of flexibility in individual prices is a prime necessity in a free and soundly functioning economic system. The judgment of the market place performs vitally important functions in encouraging needed and discouraging less needed production and in turning consumption into channels which can be readily supplied. There are limits to the utility of market-price changes. These limitations appear much more clearly in the phenomena of broad upswings and downswings of commodities as a whole than in the price movements of one commodity against another.

If producers of basic commodities were in a position to transfer freely from a less profitable to a more profitable product in accordance with the verdict of the market place, there would be an even stronger argument against interference of any kind with individual price fluctuations. But this is far from the case. A sugar colono in Cuba cannot readily begin to grow truck crops and change his entire mode of life, as soon as it appears clear that the world's sugar producing capacity is excessive in relation to other foods. The correction of such unbalanced conditions is one of the long-term objectives envisaged in the Hot Springs Food Conference,[6] but no one imagines that this will prove other than a protracted and laborious undertaking.

For these reasons we recognize that there is a necessary place in postwar planning for international agreements directed toward specific commodities which are in chronic oversupply, and that agreements of this kind may require a substantial measure of curtailment of output. As already stated, such intergovernmental agreements on a world-wide basis have been in effect, or at least initiated, with respect to wheat, sugar, coffee, rubber, and tin, and, on a more restricted scale, with respect to meat, timber, and tea.

Our proposal seeks to establish a definite relationship between these individual-commodity agreements with their *restrictive* provisions, and the broader stabilization mechanism on a commodity-unit basis, which is completely *expansionist* in its impact on the economy. In this relationship the individual-commodity agreements should play a secondary and supplementary role. Specifically, we suggest that such agreements be effective only when the commodity in question has fallen to less than 80 per cent of its moving 10-year average price, or a provisional base price in lieu thereof, and that they be suspended whenever the price has remained above 100 per cent of its average (or base) for a full year.

These agreements should be in the form recently developed for coffee and wheat, which gives substantial representation to consuming interests.[7] They may include provisions for restrictions on production, allocation of markets, creation of separate buffer stocks, etc. Every effort should be made to avoid destruction of commodities, either as part of an agreement or as a consequence thereof.[8] Some international agency, *e.g.*, the ICC, should make special arrangements to take over commodities otherwise headed for destruction. Terms could be worked out which would take such stocks completely off the commercial markets either directly or indirectly.

It is difficult to predict the extent to which special commodity agreements will be found necessary to supplement the stabilizing effect of the commodity-unit proposal. Certainly the need for such individual agreements will be greatly diminished by reason of the participation of these products in the over-all stabilization plan. Since basic unbalances correct themselves slowly, it may be assumed that in certain cases individual agreements will undoubtedly come into play.

There are a number of advantages to be realized from the interaction of the general stabilization plan and the individual commodity agreements. We have already mentioned the fact that the need for the latter should be definitely reduced. Where such steps are taken, criticism of their restrictive aspects should be allayed by the realization that they are applied only to commodities showing pronounced weakness in the face of general firmness. Placing a floor under the weaker commodities will tend to prevent excessive advances in the price of scarcer members of the composite. By reason of the "80 per cent floor" an advance in other commodities will more quickly carry the composite to the 105 per cent level, thus bringing on the sale of the entire commodity group out of the reservoir. In this way intelligent help given the weaker commodities should make for smoother and more successful operation of the general program for stability and balanced abundance.

Finally it should be pointed out that the plan proposed will prevent the giving of an excessive degree of aid to the weaker commodities. The price limits set for the operation of the individual agreements are designed to result in a somewhat lower level of prices for this group of commodities, comparatively speaking, than for those which have not required special assistance. Otherwise we may see the paradoxical result, previously alluded to, by which the parlous state of the weaker commodities is seized upon as a pretext for cartelizing them to a point which advances their price well *above* the general level. The proposed critical price level of 80 per cent of a 10-year moving average will permit small annual price declines, beginning typically at 2 per cent and gradually accelerating. Thus an *orderly* secular decline may take place in the price of perennially weak commodities, in line with underlying economic requirements.

Important Remaining Questions

In this chapter we have limited ourselves to a concise outline of our two-part proposal, *i.e.*, for both composite stabilization and subsidiary individual agreements. There has been included only as much detailed exposition and argument as seemed necessary to convey a connected and intelligible idea of the mechanism suggested. In any comprehensive economic plan such as this, there is room for an almost unlimited number of questions bearing on one or another of its aspects. We have used our judgment to select for more extended treatment in later chapters certain topics which are of primary moment in the evaluation of the entire plan. These topics will be dealt with in the following order:

1. Composite stabilization versus purchase and sale of single commodities.

2. How satisfactory is the proposed commodity unit?

3. Monetary aspects of the Commodity-reserve Plan and its bearing on the White-Keynes Plans for stabilizing foreign exchange, and on the future of gold.

4. Commodity stabilization in relation to other economic planning at the world level.

The reader will recognize that limitations of space, if not of competence, prevent us from discussing every possible ramification of our subject. We ask him in turn to give no more than proper weight to the importance of such criticisms and objections as may remain unanswered in his mind. No broad-gauge plan can be free of drawbacks; it is not to be condemned merely because it has defects, but only because these defects weigh too heavily against its accomplishments.

At this intermediate point some observations may be made with intent to simplify our task of defending the proposal against possible many-sided attack. It can be taken pretty well for granted, we think, that the buffer-stock principle must play an important part in the postwar economic world. Such buffer stocks can be created only through purchase or quasi loans amounting to purchase, as those made by our Commodity Credit Corporation. If the preceding two statements are true, then it is irrelevant to bring forward the well-known arguments against governmental purchases and sales of commodities.

Granted that such operations must interfere to a greater or lesser extent with the perfect freedom of the market, granted that they pose very difficult problems of management and financing, and granted that careful judgment exercised in one year may be proved fatuous by the capricious weather of the next—nonetheless, once the buffer-stock principle is accepted these difficulties are no longer matters of argument but troubles to contend with and to mitigate.

The argument, if there is to be any, must be carried on in the area of alternative choices within the framework of the buffer-stock concept. What shall be the underlying price policy? How wide should be the spread between buying and selling points? Are group purchases better than operations in single commodities? Must the size of the buffer-stocks be limited; if so, how? Must all purchase programs be accompanied by restriction of output? It is to these points that our attention will be directed in succeeding chapters.

Our second general observation relates to the long history and the low repute of the valorization idea. Laissez-faire economists like to stress the point that ever since governments started they have recurrently tried to fix prices and have always failed. From this they conclude that the whole concept must be patently unsound and unworkable. They seem to have given little, if any, attention to the companion question, "Why is it that, in spite of all criticisms and past failures, governments are repeatedly driven to try new valorization projects?" The obvious reason is that the state is repeatedly confronted with serious price-level difficulties which have no simple solution but which demand remedial action of some sort. Valorization thus ensues, almost by compulsion. Formerly the usual problem was to hold back rapidly *rising* prices, due to the impairment of currency values; in more recent times—between wars—the evil has often lain in an intolerably *low* price level. These crises are not disposed of by pointing out the obvious limitations of price-fixing measures; nor does the partial or even complete failure of these measures necessarily mean that the crises would have been less harrowing had they not been tried.

Furthermore, the general objective of stabilization should not be assayed solely on the basis of its performance in times of great emergency. At these junctures most of the damage has already been done, troublesome consequences are inevitable, and stabilization measures may then be called upon to perform the impossible. The only workable technique of stabilization lies in precisely the opposite direction. It must be adopted and applied not during emergencies but in advance of them; its objective must be to prevent rather than to remedy conditions of wide fluctuation and serious unbalance.[9]

The critical histories of price fixing are not too convincing in their detailed account of the subject.[10] The emphasis is always laid on measures *improvised* to prevent inevitable inflation or collapse. Little is said of the successful working of a scientific system such as the Chinese Ever-normal Granary, which apparently maintained reasonably stable prices for grain over many centuries and at the same time provided a safeguard against drought and famine. The story of Joseph in Egypt and of the seven fat and the seven lean years has passed into the homely wisdom of the ages; but our economic thinking seems to have lost contact with so simple and basic an approach to prudent management of a nation's welfare.[11]

Chapter VI

COMPOSITE STABILIZATION VERSUS INDIVIDUAL STABILIZATION

> "Experience shows that one-commodity planning invariably tends towards restriction by one or more such devices as restrictions on current output or exports, the destruction of supplies, restrictions on new productive capacity, the financing of producers so that they can withhold supplies from the market, and the allocation of markets."
> —International Labour Office.[1]

INSOFAR as our proposals contemplate the stockpiling of raw materials and their later disposal when needed, we seem to be well in line with the prevalent thinking. Many references to international planning include provision for an international commodity corporation which could act to stabilize prices by means of buffer stocks. When it comes to the mechanism itself there is room for wide difference of opinion as to how it should function. What may no doubt be termed an authoritative presentation of the semiofficial viewpoint on this subject is contained in an article by Alvin H. Hansen.[2] Virtually the entire significant reference is contained in a single paragraph, quoted herewith:

Equally important from the standpoint of preparing a world-wide attack on deflation would be the work of an international commodity corporation, designed to buy, store, and sell raw materials and to act as a buffer in the raw materials market. In the event that a deflation of raw material prices seemed to impend, the International Commodity Corporation should make large purchases of storable raw materials. It would permit the free play of market forces between upper and lower limits for each commodity. Buying operations would be indicated as soon as the price pierced the lower limit, and selling operations as soon as it rose above the upper limit. These upper and lower limits should be the subject of continuous study by the corporation and should be adjusted from time to time according to fundamental trends of normal supply and demand. An important part of the corporation's function would be to search for new uses for basic raw materials, and to cooperate with the various national governments to facilitate the movement of resources out of submarginal areas in an effort to adjust normal supply to normal demand.

It is clear from the above (and from the writer's personal discussions with leading proponents of the ICC idea) that they intend it to operate by purchase and sale of separate commodities. The plan is to acquire such products as may be in—presumably temporary—oversupply, and to dispose of them later when a suitable demand develops. Apparently a very wide discretion is proposed to be given to the managers of this agency with respect to the timing and the extent of its operations. However, a statement made to the Food Conference by an official of our State Department indicates that buffer-stock acquisitions would be confined to "a few commodities like wheat, cotton, sugar, and coffee, in which there have been heavy and long-continued surpluses in international trade during peacetime."[3]

The arguments in favor of single-commodity operations appear, at first blush, very persuasive. Setting up a commodity unit would seem to be a needless complication. If the price of wheat declines and that commodity needs help, why must we buy not only wheat, but corn, iron, etc., which might then be in scarce supply? If the weakness of wheat impels us to action, would it not be simple logic to confine that action to wheat alone?

Our answer must be that what at first appears to be the most direct and simplest approach to the problem is found on closer examination to harbor defects of the most serious kind. As a preliminary let us make the basic point that the stabilization we seek is ancillary and subordinate to the wider goal of balanced expansion of output. This is conceived, not as a series of rescue operations entered upon at irregular intervals as emergencies develop, but rather as a permanent underlying force calculated to stimulate the entire economy in the direction of greater production, greater employment, and higher incomes.

It is not feasible to encourage general production by improvised operations in weak commodities. The reason is obvious. Commodities showing individual and persistent price weakness are evidently in an unbalanced state vis-à-vis the economy as a whole. This unbalance cannot be corrected by merely buying the weak commodity; for that policy will encourage greater production of an item which is already relatively overproduced. The inevitable corollary is that price support for such weak commodities must be accompanied by some program for restricting output.

Here is the crux of the argument. Operations in individual commodities must either be unsound and dangerous, or they must be part of a curtailment scheme. If an ICC is to operate on the latter basis and if, as Assistant Secretary Acheson suggests, it is to deal only with cotton-sugar-wheat situations, then the corporation must become merely an agency of the various International Commodity Quota Agreements. We shall then have our own AAA program on a world-wide scale. There will be stockpiles, and an ever-normal granary slogan to be sure. But the controlling purpose will be to keep the stockpiles down to a minimum. Each increment in size will be viewed with disappointment and will be a signal for more drastic efforts to cut down production of the offending commodity.

The reason these growing stocks will be viewed with alarm is that they represent holdings of detached, individual, overproduced commodities. That each holding will have intrinsic value and a possible future utility is freely conceded. Experience shows that stocks of this type are not likely to be held with calm confidence and determination until the ultimate need for them arises. If the holdings continue to expand, they will be looked upon by the trade and the public as the unwelcome consequence of an unwise valorization program. If buying is suspended and the market price should fall, the indicated carrying loss will cause concern and criticism. Hence all the natural reactions on the part of those managing the operation will be toward cutting down output in order to establish a better relationship between supply and demand.

This is, of course, the actual history and sequel of our Federal Farm Board venture. It began in 1929 as a measure to assure "orderly marketing" of crops. Soon it was used to support the price of wheat and cotton in the face of both an oversupply of these products and a generally collapsing economy. As stated before, the Farm Board's holdings were liquidated in 1933 at a very heavy loss. It is true, the loss might have been much less if the stockpiles had been held for the drought years of 1934 and 1936. This very failure to carry through to a more favorable conclusion illustrates vividly the difficulties in the way of successfully managing operations of this type. From the commercial standpoint they are speculative, dangerous, and unsettling to trade. Thus managers are subject to a ceaseless barrage of criticism which is far from helpful to their judgment and their ultimate success.

The proponents of stabilization purchases on an individual commodity basis are not likely to question the above argument, except to claim that in many single instances the buying in times of weakness will fairly soon be followed by an opportunity to sell out at a profit. But for those commodities showing "heavy and long-continued surpluses" they are prepared to admit that stabilization buying will have to be tied in with quotas and production control.

On our side we do not deny that curtailment of output may be an excusable procedure in certain special cases, but we do protest vigorously against making such curtailment measures an integral part—nay, the central part—of the broad policy of stabilization. If buying to support prices is done in single commodities, this is exactly the kind of stabilization we shall have.

Let us now turn to the alternative procedure of purchasing and selling on a group or commodity-unit basis. Its advantages come from the fact that the commodity unit is a sound economic asset. Because it contains internal balance it carries with it no threat of unbalance to the agencies that own it. Hence this type of stockpile may be permitted without apprehension to grow to substantial size. (As was shown in the preceding chapter, there need be no occasion for *unlimited* growth here, since various means can be found of drawing off these basic materials into consumption.)

The embarrassing aspects of expanding stockpiles is closely related to the problem of financing them. As we have pointed out before, a balanced commodity unit could soundly be included in the reserves of central banks. If this is so, commodity-unit purchases become self-financing, just as are our Treasury's purchases of gold and silver. It is not feasible to accord this privilege to individual commodities. That would mean fixing a set price for each important material regardless of the many changing conditions which, over the years, modify the relative value of one against another. It would result in the acquisition and monetization of abnormally large amounts of certain overproduced items, and in stimulating further the output of things which are already out of balance.

There is a broader standpoint from which to consider the matter at issue. Stability and flexibility are inherently contradictory terms. Both are desirable, but each can be obtained only at the expense of the other. The test of a sound economic plan is not whether it achieves both these objectives completely—which is impossible—but whether it provides the major advantages of each at minimum cost.

The commodity-unit proposal offers flexibility of individual prices within a stable over-all value. This, we submit, is a desirable synthesis of the two objectives. Stability is most needed for the whole; flexibility is most necessary in the parts. A rise or fall in the price level of all basic commodities, or in the general level of prices, may at times fulfill a useful function, but such broad fluctuations are in the main far more mischievous than helpful. The opposite is true of changes in the *relationship* of individual prices, *i.e.*, changes within a stable over-all value. Such changes are sometimes unsound and unsettling, but in the vast majority of cases they reflect a natural and proper adjustment of prices to varying conditions of supply and demand.

Most important in this respect is the question whether such price changes are essentially self-correcting or self-aggravating—whether they tend to produce equilibrium or disequilibrium. Individual price adjustments are chiefly of the former kind. *When the general level is fairly stable*, a rise in the price of an individual commodity tends to encourage production and reduce buying, so that the factors causing the advance are rapidly corrected. Swings in the general price level itself are likely to exert a perverse influence upon the economy. Inflation or deflation feeds upon itself. The so-called natural corrective forces make themselves felt only after the movement has gone much too far and after great damage has been done.

Flexibility in individual prices has the great additional advantage of permitting *long-term* price changes to be made without interference. Any effort to stabilize separate prices must work at cross purposes with such secular adjustments. Proposals to stabilize a number of individual prices will of necessity provide for discontinuous changes in the fixed quotation, or range, to allow for these secular movements. The difficulties involved in providing both stability and corrections *by managerial policy* are, in this writer's opinion, almost insuperable.

There is no similar need to allow for secular changes in the price level of basic commodities generally. In fact, no such changes can be discerned in the price history of the past 150 years. Moreover, we are perfectly free to *define* our monetary unit as equivalent to a fixed assortment of basic materials—in which case the moderate and desirable fluctuations in various aspects of the economy will take place *around* the currency unit as so defined and fixed.

There are no inherent disadvantages of consequence in aiming at a fixed monetary value for a composite of commodities. The consequent stabilization, while far from complete, is of major value. As a derived but by no means minor consequence, we have the suitability of the commodity unit to function as physical backing for the monetary unit. This will enable us to adopt the familiar and smoothly-working gold-coinage mechanism as the specific means of stabilizing the commodity units. It will make the units self-financing, interest free, and—to the extent needed—self-liquidating. Finally, it will improve the soundness of the world's currency systems by tying them more closely to the basic things that the world not only wants but cannot do without.

By placing commodity units at the side of gold in the monetary system, we place them also at a wholesome distance from the commercial markets. Their effect upon the markets can only be in the direction of stability—to support prices where they are generally weak and to supply commodities when prices are moving upward. Hence there is no reason for the units to cause the unsettled and apprehensive feeling with which business regards the existence of large government stockpiles *subject to administrative discretion.*

Two other fundamental consequences flow from the eligibility of commodity units to serve as backing for currency. The first is that the world policy concerning the size of its stockpiles need not be controlled by financial considerations, but can be guided instead by the more fundamental emphasis on possible and desirable living standards. The second, of perhaps greater importance than the first, is that the very financial inadequacies which make it so difficult to consume the world's production in peacetime will be remedied by the process of building up the commodity-unit stockpile. Each addition to the store means a corresponding increase in the *monetary* resources of raw-materials producers, and this benefit will not be concentrated on a small segment of activity as in the case of gold mining, but instead it will be widely distributed among millions of producers everywhere.

This, then, is the argument on the positive side for preferring group purchases and group stocks to individual-commodity operations. There remains to consider the more technical objection which relates to possible scarce commodities in the unit. If copper is scarce and rising in price, would it not be both unnecessary and harmful to buy it up along with overabundant items? For the correct answer to this point it is necessary to consider for a moment how price movements normally develop in basic commodities.

The central fact here is that true shortage or scarcity is a very infrequent occurrence among world staples—and when it does occur the commodity-unit system can be availed of to relieve rather than intensify the situation. In the ordinary case, a rising price for corn or copper means merely an improved supply-demand situation. In the field of nonagricultural products, the reason is almost always found in a better demand. This development has the double result of both advancing the price and calling forth increased output. What we have then is not a scarcity but a *firmness* in the commodity.

Among agricultural products, variation in supply—due to the weather—is a more potent cause of price changes. Yet here, too, we must distinguish fairly between real shortage and a firm or strong demand. The most important farm crop in the United States is corn. Its price is often high in a year of good production because prosperous times bring a large consumption of meat. When world markets are considered, the effect of short crops is minimized by the diversification of sources of supply. Rare indeed is the occasion when the world cannot get what it needs of any commodity out of current production and carry-over. In fact, it may be doubted if there has been any real world shortage—apart from war demands and cartel manipulation—of an important commodity at any time in the past quarter century. A partial crop failure in one year is almost always followed by increased planting and a sufficient supply in the following season.

When the current year's crop is seriously deficient that fact is signalized by a higher market price for spot, or immediate, delivery than for future delivery. Under such circumstances necessary commodity-unit purchases can be made in the futures markets, at the lower price, and can thus avoid intensifying the demand for the current crop. More important than that, the existing stockpiles can readily be used to ameliorate the situation. All that needs to be done is the sale of spot holdings of the scarce commodity out of the buffer stock, and their concurrent replacement by purchases of an equivalent amount for future delivery. By this means the stockpile can be used both to relieve a short supply and to net a moderate price differential which will help pay storage charges.[4]

To make such operations feasible it is necessary that the stockpile contain suitable quantities of a fair number of different important commodities. These balanced holdings can be assured only if the purchasing policy includes products which are relatively firm as well as those which are relatively weak in price. It must not be forgotten that purchases will be made only when the commodity unit as a whole is selling somewhat under its standard price level. Hence it is not likely that any of the firmer commodities will then be quoted at levels which are dangerously high in the light of past history.

Failure to buy the firm commodities—either in the spot or futures market, whichever is cheaper—along with the weaker items would constitute a rather dangerous speculation on the later course of prices. These firm commodities are needed to balance the unit. Their very firmness may indicate not a temporary condition but a secular trend toward a higher level than formerly vis-à-vis the group as a whole. Such secular trends are part of our standard experience with any representative commodity group (see Table II). They reflect gradual changes in the underlying supply and demand conditions which control the so-called normal price.

To summarize the argument: Operations on an individual basis will lead to concentration on weak commodities, to heightened unbalance in production, to the losses and criticisms associated with valorization projects, and—by way of remedy—to increasing emphasis on crop restriction as the central part of the system. By contrast, group operations

TABLE II.—DIVERGENCES IN LONG-TERM COMMODITY PRICE TRENDS, AS SHOWN BY UNITED STATES PRICES OF 22 BASIC COMMODITIES IN 1913 AND IN 1941

Commodity	Price, cents		Per cent change 1941 from 1913	1921–1930 average price, cents
	1913	1941		
Wool (scoured)................	0.57	108.0	+89.0	116.0
Pig iron......................	1542.0	2410.0	+56.3	2150.0
Cottonseed oil................	7.3	10.4	+42.5	10.0
Flaxseed......................	136.0	188.0	+38.0	246.0
Zinc.........................	5.5	7.5	+34.5	6.3
Lead.........................	4.4	5.8	+31.8	7.0
All raw materials (*BLS index)...	(68.8)	(83.5)	(+21.4)	(96.4)
Tin..........................	44.0	52.0	+18.2	48.0
Wheat........................	85.0	98.0	+15.3	124.0
All farm products (BLS index)....	(71.5)	(82.4)	(+15.2)	(98.9)
Sugar (refined)...............	4.3	4.9	+13.9	6.1
Petroleum....................	93.0	106.0	+13.8	144.0
Corn.........................	61.0	67.0	+ 9.8	82.0
Cotton.......................	12.8	13.9	+ 8.5	20.0
Oats.........................	38.0	41.0	+ 7.9	44.0
Rye..........................	57.0	59.0	+ 3.5	91.0
Rice.........................	4.0	4.6	+ 1.5	4.6
Silk.........................	315.0	293.0	− 7.0	589.0
Coffee.......................	13.2	11.4	−13.6	18.5
Hides........................	18.4	14.5	−21.2	16.8
Barley.......................	70.0	55.0	−21.4	67.0
Copper.......................	15.3	11.8	−23.0	14.3
Cocoa........................	13.9	7.6	−45.0	9.9
Rubber.......................	82.0	22.0	−72.2	30.0

* BLS ▬ Bureau of Labor Statistics.

can be carried on with confidence in their soundness at every stage; they will supply a diversified buffer stock to meet temporary scarcity in the firmer as well as the weaker commodities; they require no restrictive schemes as an inherent element, but permit them to operate in an exceptional and subordinate capacity; and they can be made self-financing by according the status of monetary reserves to the composite units.

Parallel Proposals for Dealing in Separate Commodities

At the outset of this chapter we stated that no blueprints have been published describing in detail the *modus operandi* of the often mentioned ICC, which presumably is expected to deal in raw materials on an individual basis. We do have, however, a carefully worked out plan for a commodity corporation of this type to function within a single country. This is found in L. St. Clare Grondona's book, *Commodity Reserves for Safety and Stabilization*, published in England in 1939.

Grondona's espousal of the stockpile principle has the same logical basis as that of the present author. Our approaches to the whole subject are quite similar, with two important exceptions. Grondona proposes the buying and selling of single commodities instead of as a group, although he favors operations in a number of them simultaneously. Secondly, his separate commodity holdings are not self-financing, but will be carried by borrowing from his corporation, which will be guaranteed by the government.[5] His detailed proposal might be condensed into the following: The corporation will fix each year a base price, or datum line, for each covered commodity. This would be determined in consultation with an expert advisory committee representing importers, wholesalers, consumers, etc. For a period of at least twelve months the corporation will be ready to buy an unlimited quantity of each commodity at 90 per cent of the base price, and also to sell at 110 per cent of the base price to the extent that it holds stocks.[6]

The corporation will ultimately lower or advance its prices to reflect changes in supply and demand, but these new prices can be effective only a year after publication. The corporation will supply storage space to wholesalers who will be expected to carry a good part of the national reserves. It will sometimes buy and sell in the market at other than the

90 and 110 per cent levels, but this only to rotate its holdings or to acquire strategic stocks when so instructed by the government.[7]

Grondona deals frankly with the possibility that the corporation might be called upon to buy a huge quantity of a single commodity in one crop year. Using the wheat situation in 1938–1939 as an example he points out that the corporation might have had to purchase as high as 90 per cent of the world's excess carryover of some 600 million bushels at a cost of 100 million pounds sterling. In the aggregate he is prepared to have the corporation invest as much as 400 million pounds in acquiring three years' imports of, say, wheat, corn, wool, cotton, and rubber.[8]

Later, however, envisaging the possibility that reserves may grow too large for comfort, Grondona suggests that in such case a "system of restriction of output could be arranged with the producing interests concerned," similar to those in tin, copper, and rubber.[9] While opposed in principle to arbitrary restrictions on production, he recognizes the right of producers to apply them "if the only alternative is ruinous prices."

The principles of operation outlined in the foregoing plan might conceivably be followed by an international commodity corporation. The fixing of a maximum and minimum world price for each commodity by a committee of experts, to be effective for a year, would probably occasion much greater difficulty than the fixing of prices by a British group to apply to commodities imported into Britain. The present author is inherently sceptical of managed prices and believes that the political and economic difficulties in the way of setting these price ranges each year would prove enormous. Perhaps he exaggerates the dangers involved.

There is one vital point in which Grondona's detailed discussion appears to us to avoid realities. He apparently assumes that his plan will operate fairly evenly in all the subject commodities, and that thus it will create reserves for both national safety and for price stabilization in all of them. He does not consider the possibility that it might function with respect only to inherently weak commodities—resulting, perhaps, in the accumulation of ever-increasing quantities of one or two products, the price of which would have to be reduced in successive years.

There seems to us a real danger that this mechanism might operate as somewhat the equivalent of the Federal Farm Board in the United States, and that his corporation—whether British or International—would hold only stocks of a few basically overproduced commodities, such as wheat, cotton, sugar, and coffee. It is this danger of serious unbalance that has led us to reject the single-commodity approach in favor of the commodity unit.[10]

The reader might well inquire how Grondona has appraised the relative merits of the composite and the individual approach to stabilization. Grondona himself does not raise this question at all, but an interesting comment thereon is to be found in the prefatory remarks of Prof. R. F. Harrod. Here he considers the possibility of stabilizing the general price level instead of "a number of particular prices," and suggests that this would have to be done by buying "a sample assortment of commodities at a stated price for the sample," as under a fixed price for gold. Acknowledging that this idea is "perhaps more theoretically respectable" than individual price-fixing, he dismisses it as follows: "If we have to temper our schemes to public opinion, such a scheme must be regarded as less immediately practicable than Grondona's."[11]

More than 50 years ago the great Alfred Marshall recommended the composite plan as applied to gold and silver instead of to commodities; in other words, that paper money be issued against a fixed combination of gold and silver, permitting the price of each to fluctuate against the other. The advantages of this symmetallic arrangement were acknowledged by all the members of the Royal Gold and

Silver Commission, but the suggestion was rejected because too much time would be required to gain popular support for it.[12]

In the quiet Victorian days it was not surprising that an economic idea recognized as sound might be passed over because of its unfamiliarity to the public, but in a period "of great adjustment and rapid evolution"[13] such as the present, what was unfamiliar yesterday becomes the commonplace of tomorrow. It is perhaps a bit presumptuous to speak of the public's attitude toward economic innovations, since little, if any, effort has been made to test this question by the sampling process.[14] The world's leaders are constantly stressing the need for new approaches, and for courage and imagination in dealing with postwar problems; thus it would seem natural to expect that the public is not only resigned to, but actually eager for, some major departures from the defective techniques of the past.[15]

Let us close this section with a reference to a discussion of the composite approach by another great British economist, W. S. Jevons. Nearly 70 years ago he wrote as follows in his *Money and the Mechanism of Exchange:*[16]

Can we not invent a legal tender note which should be convertible, not into any one single commodity, but into an aggregate of small quantities of various commodities, the quantity and quality of each being rigorously defined? Thus a £100 note would give the owner the right to demand one quarter of good wheat, 1 ton of ordinary merchant bar iron, 100 pounds weight of middling cotton, 70 pounds of sugar, 5 pounds of tea, and other articles sufficient to make up its value. All of these commodities will of course fluctuate in their relative values, but if the holder of the note loses on some he will probably gain upon others, so that on the average his note will remain steady in purchasing power. Indeed, as the articles into which it is convertible are those needed for continual consumption, the purchasing power of the note must remain steady, compared with that of gold or silver, which metals are employed for only a few specific purposes.

This is an excellent statement of the underlying soundness of currency convertible into a group of basic commodities. But then Jevons also proceeds to dismiss the idea by adding:

In practice such a legal tender currency would obviously be inconvenient, since no one would wish to have a miscellaneous assortment of goods forced into his possession.[17]

It is clear that Jevons had not developed in his mind the full implications of his own idea. He had not envisaged the apparatus by which actual convertibility between currency and commodities would be effected on a large scale through the operations of specialists, which in turn would stabilize the value of currency in the hands of the ordinary holder without any need for action on his part.

May we not, therefore, with some justification invoke the mighty names of Alfred Marshall and W. S. Jevons as intellectual fathers of the concept of "commodity-symmetallism," *i.e.*, the establishment of two-way convertibility between the monetary unit and a composite of fundamental commodities?

Chapter VII

THE CRITERIA OF A SATISFACTORY COMMODITY UNIT

"Indeed as the articles into which it is convertible are those needed for continual consumption, the purchasing power of the note must remain steady, compared with that of gold and silver, which metals are employed for only a few specific purposes."

—W. S. JEVONS.[1]

OUR detailed proposal describes an initial commodity unit made up of 15 important products. It also points out that this number may be readily enlarged while the plan is in operation and suggests that such additions might conveniently be made at the rate of, say, one commodity a year beginning after completion of a test period. These suggestions imply that a unit confined to 15 commodities would be workable and satisfactory, but also that still better results are likely to be derived from the use of a larger list of items. By what facts and reasoning can these optimistic judgments be defended?

Let us begin by setting forth our concept of the criteria by which a commodity unit may properly be tested. The unit in question should meet three standards, *viz.*,

1. Stabilization of the unit must result in a reasonable degree of stability in the prices of other goods and services.

2. The unit must not be arbitrarily constituted in the sense that some commodities are unduly favored over others.

3. Assuming that the units are to qualify as monetary reserves, then the group of commodities should together supply a satisfactory basis or equivalent for currency.

Before applying these tests to our 15-commodity unit, we may be permitted a precautionary plea to mitigate the reader's severity. The issues involved are not matters of mathematical demonstration, and some minds may be less easily satisfied on these points than others. Such critics are asked to remember that there is room for great flexibility in working out our basic proposal. The choice of the number of commodities in the unit is at bottom a compromise between the conflicting objectives of administrative simplicity and adequate commodity coverage. This problem is inherent in the construction of any index number representing commodities, *e.g.*, to reflect the cost of living, or prices at wholesale, or the market level of commodity futures.[2] It may not be possible to tell in advance what number of commodities will produce the optimum result, but there is no intrinsic reason why trial and experience should not throw an increasingly helpful light on this question.

It will aid in the application of these tests to our 15-commodity unit if we describe briefly the method by which this unit was constructed. Since its primary objective is stabilization of the primary-materials sector, the choice would naturally fall upon those commodities which were important, needed stabilization, and could readily be stockpiled. Commodities are generally ranked as to importance in descending order of the monetary value either of world output or the world trade therein. Emphasis may well be claimed by the volume of world trade since it is this factor that measures a product's significance as an international commodity.

The first step was derived from the list of *primary commodities* reviewed in the League of Nations' study, "Problems of Raw Materials," published in 1937 (see Appendix I, page 142). If we take as our arbitrary criterion of first-rank importance an export total of at least 100 million dollars in 1935, we find 10 food items in this group and 11 nonfoods, including in the latter a composite of iron ore and pig iron. From these 21 products we have *excluded* butter, pork products, and beef as relatively perishable; silk, because 80 per cent of it came from the Japanese Empire and a great part of it is certain to be displaced by nylon; rice, because the major portion of the world trade therein was between Japan and its dependencies; and—provisionally—lumber, because the rather large variety of important types might complicate its stockpiling.[3] We were left with the 15 important commodities which constitute our tentative unit.

The second step concerns the relative *quantities* of each item in the unit. The natural procedure here was to make these quantities proportionate to either the total exports or the total output in some base period. Normally an average of five years or more would be used to smooth out temporary divergences. However, after some study it was found simplest—and quite suitable for the illustrative purposes of this book—to use the data for the single year 1937. Since the arguments in favor of using relative world output or of using relative world trade as the criterion were both persuasive, it seemed best to compromise the matter by according equal weight to each factor. The arithmetical data and calculations from which the composition of the unit was thus derived are shown in Table I, pages 44–45.

The final step is the choice of the *price level* for the commodity unit. As this is set higher or lower it would affect the absolute amount of each commodity in the unit, but it would not change the relative proportion of each. Hence if we start provisionally with one price level—say that obtaining in 1937—it requires only a simple percentage adjustment to change the unit over to some other level. It does not seem necessary or prudent to suggest at this time what the postwar price level for basic commodities should be. Instead we have contented ourselves with showing the construction of a 15-commodity unit on two illustrative bases—the 1937 level and the 1926 (and also the 1942) value of the unit which is a figure 20 per cent higher than the 1937 level. It will be observed that to adjust from the 1937 to the 1926 level it was only necessary to reduce each *physical quantity* in the unit by one-fifth.

The composite as set up undoubtedly lends itself to buffer-stock operations, since practically every one of the constituent commodities has actually been stockpiled for substantial periods both during and before the present war. The financial cost of storage varies with the individual commodity; this matter is given attention in Appendix III. Considering here only the physical problems of storage, we can state with confidence that the unit proposed will not present any unusual or especially troublesome problems in this regard.

The question of grades or varieties of the constituent commodities requires some mention here. In the case of certain of the products—rubber, copper, tin—a single standard or "tenderable" grade will represent the greater part of the commercial output and dealings can be confined thereto. Most of the commodities in the unit, however, occur in a fairly large number of distinct commercial types; but in each instance between two and six leading grades will be found to embrace the major portion of the annual production. A suitable acquisition policy must be developed which will result in the purchase of balanced quantities of the several important types of such commodities. This administrative problem must be met in any comprehensive scheme of stockpiling; it is similar in technical character to that of fairly dividing purchases among the important export markets. Since the world has already acquired considerable experience in the stockpiling technique, there seems no reason to anticipate serious difficulties on this score.

1. *The Unit Price and Prices in General*

Returning now to the criteria stated at the beginning of the chapter, the first point to consider is the effect of stabilizing the value of the unit upon the level of other prices. This depends in good part upon the relationship of the commodities in the unit to the general complex of goods and services making up the world's economy. That relationship has two aspects: the quantitative and the qualitative. Judging solely in terms of quantities, we shall find that our 15 commodities together represent a very significant, though by no means dominant, segment of the world's merchandise output and international trade. Viewed in conjunction with the essential nature of the stabilization problem, the unit commodities will be found to bulk very large indeed.

The statistics show that the global production of these 15 items in 1937 had a value of some 26 billion dollars— excluding Russia and China—and that the world exports thereof added over 6 billion dollars.

In measuring world production and trade we have been guided by the ruling practice in League of Nations' documents and other authoritative studies. Figures for China's output have been regularly excluded from world totals because they are mere guesses; its *export* figures are ascertainable and are therefore included in world trade and in some instances added to the total world production of the other countries. There is a wide diversity in the treatment of production figures for Russia. In most cases the League of Nations' statistics appear to consider them too doubtful to include in its world totals. For our purpose it seems best to exclude *all* the production figures of both China and Russia from our compilations since we are more interested in dependable relative quantities than in absolute totals of doubtful accuracy.

This technical detail does not in any wise imply that Russia or China is to be excluded from the stabilization program. It should be added that if new statistics are prepared which include the figures for these countries, they should not appreciably affect the composition of the unit since the totals for each commodity will be increased more or less proportionately.

World exports of all goods in 1937 totaled some 24 billion dollars, so that the unit commodities represented just a fourth of all trade. Accurate figures of world *production* of all goods are not available, but based on available data it would appear that a total of some 150 billion dollars (ex-Russia and China) would not be far out of line.[4] Hence the unit would account for between a fifth and a sixth of all goods produced.

A more logical comparison would be one between the unit commodities and all *raw materials* since finished goods consist only of processed raw materials. On this basis the proposed unit becomes much more important in quantitative terms. The 15 constituents have an annual value in the neighborhood of one-half that of *all* raw materials, excluding dairy and meat products, and nearly 40 per cent of the total including the two major nonstorable groups. These ratios would apply, in approximate fashion, both to global output and to the United States separately (see Appendix I).

If we turn now to the structural aspects of the stabilization problem, we shall see that the commodities in the tentative unit together cover most of the key positions in this area. It should first be pointed out that *finished goods* do not furnish any significant problem of instability *independent of fluctuations in raw-materials prices*. The statistical data show clearly that all considerable changes in the finished goods level occur later and are much smaller, percentagewise, than the swings in basic commodities. Anyone familiar with the way business affairs are conducted will recognize that there is a strong element of inertia inherent in finished-goods prices, and that it arises basically from the fact that people accustomed to do business with each other will more readily repeat a transaction at an unchanged than at a changed price.

Various factors do, of course, make for variations in these prices. In scattered instances the moving cause may be the sudden decision or whim of one concern in a competitive field. Broad changes in the finished group *of a short-term or cyclical character* will occur only if induced by a substantial change in an important element of cost. In virtually every case such a change will occur first in the raw-materials factor. The more extended the analysis along these lines, the more conclusive the proof that short-term instability in the finished-goods field is impossible without a preceding movement in raw materials. Consequently an adequate degree of stability in primary goods is certain to be accompanied by sufficient stability in processed goods.[5]

Among the raw materials, in turn, some products are relatively less stable than others, but it is a numerically small group that might properly be termed the focus of instability. This comprises the great international staples which are dealt in on commodity exchanges. They constitute an important fraction of the exports of many countries and even represent an important part of the total economy of certain nations. The nature of the market for these commodities has made their price hypersensitive to economic crosscurrents. Their structure of production has made short-term adjustments of supply to demand impossible and long-term adjustments extremely difficult. Their key position in national economies has given major and reverberating significance to the resultant wide swings in their exchange value.

TABLE III.—RAW MATERIALS OF MAJOR IMPORTANCE WHICH HAVE BEEN SUBJECT TO INTERNATIONAL AGREEMENTS OR SIGNIFICANT INTERNAL CONTROLS

A Intergovernmental agreements	B International agreements by producers	C Internal controls (excluding those under A)
Beef	Coal	Corn
Coffee	Coffee	Cotton
Rubber	Iron and steel products	Milk
Sugar	Wood pulp	Petroleum
Timber		Rice
Tin		Silk
Tobacco		Wool
Wheat		

A simple and pragmatic way of identifying these key commodities is by listing the raw products which have been subject to international price agreements or to important internal measures for restricting production. Both of these approaches to stability involve so many difficulties and objections that they obviously would not be resorted to except to mitigate an evil of the first magnitude. The appended list of commodities so affected presents interesting evidence of the aptness of our proposed commodity-unit for its intended purpose. Practically every commodity in our 15 has been subject to such stabilization measures. Only a handful of *other* major products have also been subject to such measures (Table III, page 78).

There is nothing particularly strange about this coincidence. We naturally selected for our unit the storable commodities which bulked largest in international trade. These commodities being both important and price sensitive, it was equally natural that they—and not others—should be the object of stabilization efforts.

It may be fairly claimed, we think, that the 15 commodities suggested represent a reasonably comprehensive selection from the standpoint of over-all stabilization requirements. More detailed study will doubtless result in various changes in our list, including quite probably a gradual increase in the total number of items. Sound sense might dictate that the plan be started with the lesser number of commodities and that the group be gradually expanded in the light of practical experience.

2. *Relative Treatment of the Commodities in the Unit*

Although the meticulous economist could readily pick flaws in our method of determining the relative quantity of each constituent product, and although a better technique than ours can no doubt be devised, we are certain that none will be found that is immune to all sound criticism. This matter is of more importance on the surface than it is in its deeper meaning. Brief attention will be given to the following three observations:

First, the real need here is only for a broad proportionality and not for finely calculated precision. Second, the arithmetical technique can be improved as we go along and serious faults, if any, readily corrected. Third, our approach to proportionate dealings, which is at least quasi-scientific, is certain to result in fairer treatment between commodities than any stockpiling policy based only on human judgment and day-to-day emergencies.

Once we admit the need for international stockpiling of *some* commodities we pass from the realm of abstract desirability into merely practical questions. By one means or another a decision will have to be reached as to how much wheat will be acquired as against how much corn. The problem here is not nearly so difficult as others which have already been met and surmounted in international commodity arrangements and cartels. In those instruments, each relating to a single staple, it was necessary to agree upon the allocation of world exports—and perhaps world production— among competing nations. The percentage figures arrived at were of vital importance to the nations concerned because in most cases they controlled the whole productive pattern for a dominant commodity. Nor was the mathematical basis for allocation an obvious one; for example, a country with a good trend of recent growth would not show up well statistically on the basis of, say, a five-year average.[6]

Despite the many possible bases of disagreement on these allocations, it has been possible to work them out by discussion and give-and-take negotiation in the case of dozens of commodities.

By contrast, the relative amount of each commodity in the unit is a matter of much smaller concern to the producers. Purchases of *complete units* in any one year will comprise only a very minor portion of the total output; 5 per cent would be an unusually high figure, we believe. This is naturally much smaller than the proportion of the year's output of certain *single* commodities that might be acquired if efforts were made to stabilize weak commodities separately. Hence even if the quantity of one material in the unit were set as much as 20 per cent lower than it deserved, this "unfair" treatment might mean only that 1 per cent less of the production than justified would be acquired in a given year. Furthermore, this minor disadvantage might well be offset in subsequent years when the units were being disposed of in a rising market. At that time the undermeasured commodity will benefit through having a correspondingly smaller amount sold out of the stockpile in competition with current production.

3. *Suitability as Backing for Money*

The same reasoning applies to this aspect of the commodity unit when viewed as a possible monetary equivalent. It is desirable that the group of basic commodities be comprehensive and well-balanced. Three-decimal-place exactitude is of no special value here. Until our economic life grew overcomplicated, we managed quite well with money directly convertible into only one or two metals, which in turn had only a roundabout utility in terms of the daily needs of mankind. If now we place in addition a group of primary goods behind the world's money, it is not remotely necessary that each person's dollar be redeemable in the precise goods, and in their precise proportions, that correspond to his individual needs. The fact is that even a very crudely fashioned commodity unit will probably supply a satisfactory physical backing for paper currency. It is necessary to avoid extreme unbalance as, for example, a money backed solely by coffee, or a "unit" consisting 95 per cent of copper and 5 per cent of minor amounts of many other commodities.[7]

On this point we should like to put forward as a thesis *the principle of equivalence of useful goods*. By this we mean that any fund of goods which are unquestionably valuable to a nation or nations may be considered as economically equivalent, on a fair basis, to other valuable goods. In *Storage and Stability* we applied this thesis in defense of the utility of commodity units as suitable assets of a Social Security Reserve Fund, in the following language:[8]

Speaking concretely, if we assume that the beneficiaries of the Social Security Act had a fund consisting of basic commodities, all of which were useful, this fund would have the same financial value to them, and the same economic value to the nation, as if it consisted of the actual manufactured goods which they could be expected to consume. For in the ordinary economic process a free and desirable interchange could take place between the raw commodities which they held and the manufactured goods which they want. This idea does not imply that an unlimited supply of a single useful commodity would do as well as our commodity units. For the supply of the single commodity might be so disproportionate to that of other commodities entering into consumption that its economic value was thereby greatly diminished. Our diversified commodity unit avoids this serious pitfall.

This reasoning, we believe, holds true with respect to the basic utility of commodity units for all purposes, provided they comprise a reasonably representative market basket of primary materials.

Chapter VIII

COMMODITY STABILITY AND CURRENCY STABILITY

"What matters most to the rest of the world is that the United States should enjoy a stable prosperity without any disturbing fall in the price level and without alternate booms and slumps, which spread havoc far outside American boundaries and by themselves would suffice to wreck any international currency scheme."
—*The Times*, London, Apr. 22, 1944.

INTRODUCTORY SUMMARY

OUR projected world currency based on commodity units bears an important relationship to the pending proposals for international currency stabilization which first appeared under the names of the Keynes and White plans. These have now progressed into the stage of preliminary agreement on the technical level embodied in what we shall call the Experts' plan.[1] To add clarity to the discussion of what is at best an intricate subject, we shall state here in outline form the four main points which will be developed in this chapter.

1. The International Monetary Fund, set up in the Experts' plan, can be the agency not only for international credit operations but for commodity-reserve currency operations as well. The two concepts can supplement each other to a valuable extent, and they can be made effective by a single mechanism.

2. The Experts' plan deals not with price-level stability but stability of foreign-exchange rates. It proposes to maintain this stability by credit operations, *i.e.*, by lending of "international money" from creditor nations to debtor nations. By contrast, the issuance of commodity-reserve currency is not a credit operation but a coinage operation.

83

The commodity-reserve device will reduce, but not obviate, the need for extending international credits. It will thus protect the IMF in part, against the danger of issuing an excessive amount of unsecured credits to borrowing nations.

3. Commodity-reserve currency will occupy the same formal position as gold in the field of international money. Generally speaking, it will place raw-materials nations in the same position as gold-producing nations. Thus it will supplement gold but not replace it.

While gold has a useful function to perform, its future monetary position, like that of silver, is likely to be based more upon convention than unquestioned intrinsic worth. This position would be threatened by world economic instability and severe depression. If commodity-reserve currency will promote stability and expansion in the world economy—as we claim—it will thus protect the somewhat precarious status of gold. However, the present price of $35 per ounce may be unsound in relation to the existing price level. If prices can be stabilized around this level, it might be well to reduce the price of gold.

4. Commodity-reserve currency has certain basic superiorities to both gold and international credits. It embodies the new attitude of *groceries first*. To this end it can bring the world's financial economy closer to its merchandise economy and prevent world finance from interfering with the true business of the world which is to produce, exchange, and consume useful goods and services.

Commodity-reserve Money and Currency Stabilization

A stable price level for commodities implies, by definition, a stable value for the currency in which prices are measured. To that extent commodity stability is synonymous with currency stability. Our proposed international commodity-reserve currency will therefore result in a stable international money of account. This may be expressed in terms of a special unit (such as bancor or unitas), in American dollars, or in a given weight of gold. We have hitherto discussed the stable level of commodity prices in terms of dollars. As long as we consider the price of gold to be fixed at $35 per ounce, a stable dollar price level and a stable gold price level mean the same thing. If we expect the dollar value of gold to change we have a complication to be considered later.

In comparing the world currency envisaged in the Experts' plan with our commodity-reserve currency, a basic distinction must be made at the outset. The White and Keynes plans have dealt with the stabilizing of foreign-exchange rates; their specific objective has been merely to fix the relative value of one national money against another. This is by no means equivalent to stabilizing the world price level of commodities; we all know that price levels have fluctuated disturbingly even while the important foreign-exchange rates have remained substantially constant. Conversely, it is possible, though not likely, that prices may remain stable in terms of gold or dollars while the quoted value of the pound or franc may change radically.

Although foreign-exchange stability and price-level stability are not related by definition they have a kinship of a practical kind. Wide instability in either area is likely to be a threat to the other; reasonable stability in both is considered necessary to the future prosperity of the world. Hence both the White and Keynes plans, as published, carried references to the desirability for complementary action in the field of raw materials. In Secretary Morgenthau's foreword to the United States Treasury's proposal, he states that "Other agencies may be needed to provide long-term credit for post-war reconstruction and development; to provide funds for rehabilitation and relief; and to promote stability in the prices of primary international commodities."[2] Such agencies, he suggests, should be separate from the IMF, which is to concentrate upon stability of the exchanges.

Lord Keynes envisaged a closer relationship between his Clearing Union and the stabilization of commodities. The text of the British plan, dated Apr. 8, 1943, contains a section discussing "additional purposes of high importance and value which the union, once established, might be able to serve." The third of these reads as follows:

> The union might set up an account in favor of international bodies charged with the management of a commodity control, and might finance stocks of commodities held by such bodies, allowing them overdraft facilities on their accounts up to an agreed maximum. By this means the financial problem of buffer stocks and ever-normal granaries could be effectively attacked.[3]

Moreover the fifth additional purpose mentioned in this section pertains to the use of the Clearing Union's powers "to maintain stability of prices and to control the trade cycle." For this object Keynes envisages the setting up of three supplementary agencies, *viz.*, an International Economic Board, an International Investment or Development Corporation, and finally a "scheme of commodity controls for the control of the stocks of staple primary products."

Our own suggestions would endow the buffer stocks of commodities with a concrete monetary character and function. In this respect we go beyond the Keynes idea, quoted above—which, incidentally, is advanced as a possible but not a necessary utilization of the general scheme for a clearing union—and, of course, we depart considerably from the outline of the American currency plan. Yet it will be seen that our underlying philosophy of basing money supply in part on physical holdings of primary commodities is really closer to the American than to the British concept of international money, and thus closer to the terms of the Experts' plan, which is built largely upon the philosophy of the White proposals.

Because commodity-reserve currency is essentially a method of dealing with merchandise, it fits naturally into the underlying concept of foreign trade—which is the mutual exchange of merchandise and services. To the extent that this fails to happen, the world resorts to second-best devices, such as shipments of gold and the extension of credits. Both the Keynes and the White plans were measures to make available credits, called international money, which presumably would not be supplied by private banking operations. For this very reason the inherent soundness of such credits must be open to some degree of question at least, and the proposed operations may have to be justified on the ground of their collateral benefits. This fact removes them one step farther from the simple virtues of an even trade of merchandise.

Where adverse trade balances occur, the best means of settling them may lie neither in gold shipments nor in granting credits. It may be sounder to reexamine the merchandise situation and to see whether it is not possible for the debtor country to marshal or to earmark *goods* to balance the account, even though the goods are not at that moment wanted by the creditor nations. Gold has functioned as an ever-wanted merchandise, but only because in modern times it has never had to enter the channels of trade or seek out buyers or compete with other goods. What may be needed to facilitate world trade is not so much the widening of the field of international *credits*, but rather the extension of the preferred status of gold to cover other products of much greater inherent usefulness. In other words, instead of "the generalization of the principle of commercial banking,"[4] rather a generalization of the principle of gold settlements. This can be done quite ideally through the commodity-unit device.

As this chapter is written it is by no means certain that the Experts' plan, or anything similar, will be put into effect. For purposes of discussion, let us assume such adoption and ask an initial question: "Are the commodity-unit and the currency-stabilization plans mutually exclusive, complementary, or entirely independent in their scope?" We shall answer that the two ideas are in no wise antagonistic; that they are basically complementary; but that they can be viewed and acted upon as separate entities.

Critiques of the Keynes and White plans have appeared in such profusion that any detailed exposition here—even of the successor product—would be quite superfluous.[5] Let us merely repeat that the plans propose to maintain stable exchange rates by advancing funds to debit-balance countries, thus enabling them to meet their payments. Such advances will be limited in their total amount and subject to other conditions. In the newest proposal, each currency value will be fixed in terms of gold and thus fixed in terms of every other participating currency. There are provisions for orderly changes in these gold values where required.

The IMF will have a capital of some 9 billion dollars, contributed in gold and local currencies. In the typical operation it will make its advances by turning over a needed local currency, or gold, in exchange for the currency of the debtor nation. If we envisage a persistent one-way movement of trade balances, say in favor of the United States against all other nations, the IMF will gradually turn back to us the gold we contributed plus the rest of its initial gold. Its capital will then be represented by holdings of the currencies of the debtor nations in place of the gold with which it started. If, however, the member nations alternate as debtors and creditors on current account, then the assets of the fund will vary in their make-up from time to time, and its function may be fulfilled without a permanent trend toward replacing better assets by poorer ones.

The commodity-unit proposal does not involve advances by the IMF to debtor nations, but the other way around. A nation selling commodity units or components entering into such units to the IMF is exactly like one that sells gold to the IMF. It turns over a physical asset in exchange for a deposit credit, which it can thenceforth use as money. The essential result of the commodity-unit mechanism is thus to diminish the need for advancing money from the fund to debtor nations. By supplying parts of commodity units they can pay their trade balances with them and thus keep out of debt. The credit machinery of the IMF will have to operate only to the extent that the nations do not have available raw materials which can be combined into commodity units.

We do not at all assume that the monetizing of commodity units will solve all the problems of debit-balance nations. In many cases countries will either be unable to produce a surplus of component raw materials with a value equal to their import balance or else they will be loath to increase the output of one or two major products because thereby the individual price will be unduly depressed. It is not necessary that a nation produce and tender complete commodity units. It is necessary, however, that each nation's production of component commodities fit reasonably well into the *world* output of complete units. In many instances, therefore, the credit mechanism set up in the IMF will serve a useful purpose.

The two arrangements combined should supplement each other ideally. The commodity-unit device will greatly facilitate the attainment of long-run equilibrium for the many raw-materials nations which lack inherent financial strength. It will thus obviate for them those acute cyclical or short-term problems which arise from recurrent collapse in the price structure. As our opening quotation from the *London Times* makes clear, even the powerful United States is highly vulnerable to such price collapses, and they have power to wreck any currency scheme. On the other hand, the credit or loan machinery will smooth over temporary rough spots in international finance and afford breathing spells for nations needing to work out gradually an over-all balancing of their foreign-trade position.

This cheerful statement that there is room for both commodity-reserve currency and credit operations to function side by side within the IMF will hardly dispose of a question which has aroused so many conflicting reactions. It seems necessary, therefore, to develop some aspects of the problem in greater detail. As we see it, the proposals under discussion really envisage three kinds of international money: (*a*) gold, (*b*) the capital and deposits of the IMF (in general similar to White's unitas and Keynes' bancor), and (*c*) commodity-unit currency. In commenting on the threefold relationship here involved we have three points to make, *viz.*,

1. From the American approach the credit operations of the IMF are likely to work out mainly as another means—fifth of a series—of paying us for our export balances with something less valid than usable goods and services. This characterizes but does not condemn the scheme, since an imperfect solution of our export-balance problem is better than none at all.

2. It would not be impossible to maintain our export-balance position by simply accepting most of the world's annual production of gold in payment. The greater our confidence in the intrinsic value of gold the more reason to proceed in this time-honored fashion. However, this solution is incompatible with the objectives of the White plan (and its successor), which clearly seeks to validate gold internationally by offering other countries credit concessions in return for their renewed allegiance to gold. This eagerness suggests a certain mistrust on our part of the real worth of gold considered apart from its formal recognition in a world banking system.

3. The new economic philosophy subordinates money to the production of useful goods and services. If this concept is sound it should express itself also in the field of international currency. It would attach a special merit to commodity-unit currency because this currency identifies money with useful merchandise. In this respect commodity units are clearly better things for a creditor nation to own than claims against a IMF, and their value is less ambiguous than that of gold. Conversely, commodity units will afford every country the opportunity to transmute its own productivity into sound international monetary units free from demoralizing fluctuations in exchange value.

These three points will be developed in the next chapter.

Chapter IX

COMMODITIES, GOLD, AND CREDIT AS WORLD MONEY

"The stability of the Soviet currency is secured primarily by the tremendous volume of commodities in the hands of the State, and placed in circulation at stable prices. What economist can deny that such security is more real than any gold reserve?"
—JOSEPH STALIN, 1933.[1]

THE many published critiques of the White and Keynes plans indicate how wide apart is the thinking of our foremost economists on the monetary problems of today. Conservative writers, like Benjamin Anderson, have branded both plans as mischievous contrivances which disguise and will later aggravate evils that need a drastic cure.[2] Viner considers a general scheme of the kind proposed quite essential to the postwar economy, although he is very discriminating in his appraisal of detailed provisions.[3] Neisser favors the British plan for purposes of an international reserve bank but likes the paid-in capital idea to assist in financing world trade. In direct contrast to the views of our gold-standard advocates he insists that the fixed value of gold provided in the White plan is disadvantageous to the United States but helpful to the British Empire and Russia.[4] On the other hand, F. A. Lutz says flatly, "Gold is quite unnecessary or even a nuisance under both schemes."[5]

Some clue to this divergence of views may appear when we relate them to the kind of foreign-trade balances that the various critics are expecting to appear in the postwar world. One view is certain that a number of weak nations will for a long while be compelled to import more merchandise than they could possibly export. On this basis the need would be not for an ambitious credit scheme but for carefully supervised aid through relief and rehabilitation agencies. A second view is that the so-called debtor nations could readily balance their accounts if only other countries—chiefly the United States—would lower tariffs and accept their goods. If this is so, the extension of bancor credits is fundamentally a sound risk since the export-balance nations are free to turn these credits into merchandise whenever they are ready to buy it. Keynes himself has gone even farther and insisted that even under present tariffs the United States would not run up a substantial export balance when conditions are reasonably prosperous. Therefore he is quite confident that the volume of bancor balances should prove self-limiting and possibly self-liquidating.[6]

This last view has been received with considerable skepticism. Even the London *Economist* says bluntly, "It has never been easy, ever since the last war, for countries other than the United States to earn as many dollars as they require; but it will be very much more difficult after the war."[7] During the six years 1934–1939 the merchandise export balance of this country averaged 500 million dollars per annum. In the absence of a striking change in tariff policy we might expect our postwar credit balance for goods and services to run not less than this figure and very possibly as high as a billion dollars a year.[8]

More plausible is the view expressed by Keynes that even if we accumulate a large volume of bancor this is no different from an ordinary bank deposit and can be drawn on to buy merchandise abroad whenever we elect to do so. Yet in two serious respects the analogy with ordinary commercial banking is inexact: first, banks lend only with careful attention to the soundness of the loan, and, second, their own capital is at first risk to meet losses through unwise credits. In the bancor scheme there is, of course, no stockholders' capital to take the first loss. What is equally important, the extension of credits to nations will not depend upon the application of ordinary banking tests of credit-worthiness. A very large sum will be made available as a matter of right—in Keynes's language, as "a once-for-all endowment."[9] He adds that it is most important to see that improvident countries do not run through their allotment, but as yet there does not appear to be any sure and simple method of preventing such an abuse of confidence.

It is not so easy in practice as it may seem in theory for a chronic-creditor nation to spend its fund deposits on goods. Claims against the IMF may be for either contributed capital or deposits. For convenience we shall refer to them as IMF deposits, or merely as claims or credits. These credits, unlike typical bank deposits, will not be held by specific firms or individuals who can dispose of them at will. American-owned claims against the IMF will be assets of the Federal Reserve Banks or the United States Treasury or both. These owners cannot spend them for merchandise. Nor will the creditors of these owners—the bank depositors and government bondholders in the United States—have any individual reason to spend these claims or any particular means of so doing.

In other words, even if our country (*i.e.*, the economists or the man in the street) recognized that it would be sound policy to turn our IMF deposits into goods, there would be no way to bring this about except through such changes in our tariff policy as would finally lead impersonally to an excess of imports. Granted that such a drastic move toward free trade would be desirable, its chance of adoption would still be small, for the simple reason that those manufacturers who would lose severely through lower tariffs will work ten times as hard to oppose them as theoretical economists will work to bring them about.

If we view the Keynes-White proposals realistically, we are likely to conclude that they would work out as the fifth of a series of devices operating since 1917 for paying the United States for its merchandise exports with a substitute for merchandise. Prior to 1920 we took war debts; in the 1920's our private investors bought foreign bonds; in the 1930's the means of payment was gold; in the Second World War

period there are Lend-Lease obligations; in the postwar years
the proposed medium will be IMF credits. The first three
methods of settlement have occasioned much criticism and
dissatisfaction both inside and outside this country. We have
had to write off nearly all the war debts and a large proportion of the subsequent loans abroad. Ours has been a good
share of the fault—partly through an under-generous attitude toward the war debts, partly through an unwise
eagerness to lend later at high rates of interest, and always
through our unwillingness to import freely. The golden
avalanche of the 1930's, like the experience of the Sorcerer's
Apprentice, became much too much of a good thing, and all
but culminated in the complete discrediting of gold itself.[10]
It is safe to predict that the Lend-Lease arrangement will
come in for a large share of political attack before its books
are closed, although we may hope to handle this phase with a
reasonable show of dignity and magnanimity.

In the last 30 years we have exported some 50 billion
dollars more of merchandise than we imported. This is a
colossal figure, yet there is no indication that it impoverished
us in any way. If in the future the urge to export on balance
still afflicts us—as it probably will—we can afford to indulge
it, even though the payment we receive in exchange may
prove of dubious value. The international-fund scheme is
not necessarily condemned by pointing out that we shall
probably use it so as *not* to get a full *quid pro quo* for our
exports.

While the alternatives are not so simple as Lord Keynes
describes them, we do have the ultimate choice under the
IMF of either continuing our export balances or evening up
our trade. Even if we place the most cynical construction
on the credit plans and assert that they do nothing but
create a large amount of purely illusory international wealth,
it might be pointed out that the quantity of similarly
illusory wealth within nations is far greater (*cf.* bank deposits
backed by government bonds), and yet its effects are not
only tolerable but perhaps even helpful.

The Gold-import Alternative

As an alternative, at least theoretically practicable, to amassing IMF credits, the United States could elect to continue to receive the greater part of the world's gold production, which in recent years amounted to some 1.5 billion dollars annually. This would be a very neat solution of the problem, provided we assume (*a*) that the rest of the world can handle its trade balances except for the American exports, and (*b*) that we would be willing to accept gold even though most of the other countries no longer used it for money.

The first assumption may not be entirely accurate, but it gives us a fairly good working hypothesis. Certainly, if the export balance of the United States could be readily settled, the remaining problems of international trade should shrink to manageable proportions. The question thus comes down to the attitude of this country toward gold, independent of the behavior of the rest of the world. If gold were as desirable in and for itself as the pure gold-standard advocates contend, then this should be no problem at all. We should be glad to obtain as much of it as possible, regardless of the position of other nations. Cornering 90 per cent of the world's gold would be no more disadvantageous to us than owning that proportion of the world's helium—which we do—or of the world's copper or petroleum.

Our eagerness to see that other countries possess gold and use it in their own monetary systems is a strong indication of our doubt of its intrinsic value. The writer shares this doubt, but he considers it nonetheless a misfortune for the world of today. If gold would continue to be universally accepted as money without question or limitation, the problems of settling postwar trade balances would be greatly simplified, even though, paradoxically, we might be the only important country which actually based our money on gold. The United States Treasury's currency plan—now the Experts' plan—appears to be as much a rescue operation for gold as it is for debtor countries. It offers the world a certain amount of credit on condition that they recognize the present value of gold as inviolable. By contributing a substantial portion of their gold holdings as part of the capital of the IMF, all gold-owning nations will assume a permanent stake in the future of gold—at least to the extent that they could not unload all their gold on the United States if they felt they would rather have dollars or merchandise instead.

One of the back-handed advantages of the war has been its contribution toward solving the problem of redistributing our gold holdings throughout the world. As in the First World War the heavy imports and curtailed exports of the active belligerents resulted in a substantial flow of gold to secondary nations. Instead of our having some 85 per cent of the monetary gold of the world—as was calculated a few years ago—the situation at the end of 1943 shows us with two-thirds of the global gold supply and the balance of 11 billion dollars quite widely scattered.[11] This would suggest that enough nations will have a substantial interest in gold after the war to make practicable the establishment of a fairly widespread international gold standard.

It would appear, however, that the price of $35 per ounce is too high in relation to the general price level now current in the United States. Unless we are to have a plateau of prices after the war substantially above the present average it would seem most sensible to reduce the buying price for gold to somewhere around $25 per ounce. At that figure production might recede to less disturbing levels, other nations would more readily pay over goods for gold, and we ourselves would view with more equanimity a steady annual influx. The loss from devaluation of our gold holdings, being a bookkeeping item, can be handled in bookkeeping fashion by continuing to carry our gold stocks at cost. This would place gold in precisely the same formal monetary position as that of silver.[12]

No plan for the future of the gold will command even an approximation to universal consent. Despite the apparent acceptance of gold as the world currency base by the experts of all the United Nations, it is by no means certain that the arrangements will actually be put into effect and continued through the difficult years ahead.[13] The still unsettled position of gold lends especial point to our suggestion that international money be related *also* to basic raw materials. We believe that this arrangement will assist greatly in stabilizing both the monetary and the commodity structure of the world. Incidentally, it will make far easier the maintenance of whatever status is finally given to gold.

Commodity-unit currency is physical money. It belongs in the tradition and conforms to the discipline of the classic gold standard. Professor Hayek, long a vigorous defender of the gold standard, has pointed out[14] that new conditions in the world call for a broader standard which will produce more rapidly and helpfully the compensatory effects upon the economy which had theoretically followed from the workings of the gold mechanism. Accumulation of gold during periods of high liquidity preference, and stimulus to gold mining during period of falling prices, carried comparatively little advantage to the great structure of production. Under such conditions similar operations in the reserve commodities would exert a prompt and beneficial influence on a major sector of the economy and would supply nations with a valuable increment to their real wealth.

The advantage that commodity-reserve currency on an international scale will give to all raw-materials exporting nations is obvious. Broadly speaking, it endows their shipments of these products with the status of gold exports. It is not necessary that a single country have complete commodity units for sale in order to benefit from the stable demand for the units. Each land can contribute what it has to offer; the impersonal and efficient machinery of the world's markets will combine into rounded units these offerings from many quarters. Since the value of each item is subject to variation there will be changes—now unfavorable, now favorable—in the relative share of different products in the combined selling price. As long as production of the components is kept in fairly sound balance there should not be any disturbing revolutions in the economic position of one against the other. Of overshadowing importance is the fact that *balanced expansion in all the items collectively* can proceed unabated without the familiar and disastrous consequences of price collapse. This is the basic goal of all postwar planning.

For emphasis we repeat our earlier statement that commodity units are not put forward as a formal substitute for the Monetary Fund. A nation which may owe money on current account will not necessarily be able to produce additional raw materials as components in sufficient quantity to settle its balances. The units will expand the world's supply of international currency, and they will facilitate the settlement of international balances by many countries. In this they will operate precisely as an addition to current gold production by the participating nations. The problem of extending a certain amount of international credit will still remain, and here the Monetary Fund operations may serve a useful and unique purpose.

Except for a suggestion made below, it does not seem necessary to indicate here what in our opinion would be the most satisfactory *modus operandi* of such a credit agency. All will agree that the smaller the scale of activity required of it, the better. Even under the best circumstances money lending among nations is apt to cause more grief than satisfaction. By giving many countries additional means of payment through their production of raw materials, the commodity-reserve mechanism may reduce the scope of international credit operations to a range well within our capacity of intelligence and good will.

Viner, in his careful analysis of the two currency plans, pronounces against the inclusion therein of "credits for ever-normal granary schemes,"[15] etc., as suggested by Keynes. However, Viner's criticism is directed against the combination of unrelated functions in a single agency; he assumes, with justice, that the commodity stabilization measures envisaged by Keynes would bear no organic relationship to the international monetary machinery. Under our proposal commodity units would function in the same way as gold vis-à-vis bancor or IMF deposits and would thus become a constituent part of the world's monetary organization.

An expanding world economy can deal with all its problems much more easily than a contracting one. Trade barriers will fall more quickly; foreign investments can develop more satisfactorily; and the very peace of the world is more readily maintained. The same beneficent effect will be found upon the status of gold. As the stabilization plan takes final shape we are likely to see emerge a constellation of attitudes toward gold combined into a single formalized position. This will recognize the real devotion of some people to gold, the traditional acceptance by others, the political pressures of still others—and also the great practical utility of gold as an international counter or "poker chip." Whatever this position will be, it is not likely to rest on too firm a base. Like other conventional and convenient arrangements it will need surrounding stability for its survival. To the extent that commodity reserve currency can contribute toward an expanding and reasonably stable world economy it will contribute also toward maintaining the conventionalized status of gold.

Commodity-unit Currency and International Bimetallism

Advocates of silver as a formalized world currency have recently renewed their familiar plea for international bimetallism. Their chief argument is the need for a medium of payment in addition to gold. This was voiced by an influential silverite in the following paragraph:

If a plan like the White or Keynes schemes is ultimately adopted, therefore, every practical measure should be taken to increase the ability of a nation to maintain its credit balance on the books of the International Stabilization Fund, and thus the stability of its currency, even though its balance of international payments turns unfavorable for a considerable period of time. This calls for an expansion of the volume of settlement media beyond the limit imposed by the amount of gold available.[16]

Our commodity-unit proposal is clearly identical in its *formal* character with that of the silver advocates. We suggest that a composite of commodities be given the same monetary position as they wish be given to silver. We, too, point out that by so doing the import-balance nations will find it easier to even up their accounts.

Conservative economists condemn the silver movement as an attempt by a limited pressure group to revive a discredited metal. Many progressive economists insist that gold is now in essentially the same position as silver and that the arguments the simon-pure gold advocates use against the white metal can be directed with equal effect against their own fetish. Be that as it may, we shall content ourselves with the assertion that commodity symmetallism is basically superior to bimetallism, for four important reasons. First, it relates money to the sound value of many necessary goods and not to a largely factitious value imparted to one favored commodity. Second, it will increase the supply of standard money more generously than can be done by coining silver alone, and it will spread the coinage advantages over many more nations and millions more individual producers. Third, it will contribute directly to stabilizing the price level of basic raw materials and to stimulating a balanced expansion in their output. Fourth, it will create truly useful reserve stocks of such materials, which can minister to the safety and prosperity of the world.

Effect of an International Price Level upon National Policies

Proposals dealing with world objectives invariably raise questions as to their effect upon internal policies and they are almost invariably attacked because they limit national freedom of action. The plans for currency stabilization have been no exception. Many of the reservations expressed in the parliamentary debates with respect to the Keynes and White proposals were centered on the danger that by directly or indirectly tying the pound to gold the British would lose their ability to deal with internal problems by monetary means. More specifically, there was fear that deflation and depression in the United States would be transmitted to England *via* the inflexible currency relationship.[17]

The same question must arise when we are dealing with methods of stabilizing the international price level of primary products as a group. Would such a plan limit the ability of England to cut itself loose from an American depression? Would it also interfere with the ability of the United States Department of Agriculture to carry out the congressional mandate to support crop prices at 90 per cent of "parity" for two years after the close of the war? What, in short, would be the relationship between the international mechanism and national price policies?

The basic answer here is that an international commodity-reserve currency does not bind any nation to do or not to do anything within its borders. It is solely a buying and selling system applicable to a limited group of commodities, under which the products are at times bought and stored and at other times disposed of in the world's markets. Any limiting effect of this arrangement on national policies must therefore be an indirect and derived one. What we are doing is substituting an unchanging world level for raw materials for one that fluctuates widely. The problem of adjusting any desired national policy to a stable world level will be no different *in its formal character* than it was before; but in its *substantive* character the problem should be much simpler than before because, generally speaking, national economic objectives can be more readily attained against a background of stable than of widely changing world prices.

To be concrete, let us first consider the United States policy of maintaining its farm prices at 90 per cent of parity for some years to come. The commodity-unit plan will aim at a closely similar result for world prices; hence execution of the congressional mandate would undoubtedly be aided by the international mechanism. If, on the contrary, world

agricultural prices were permitted to collapse—as in 1921—
the American program would be far more difficult to carry
out.

Suppose, however, that within the stabilized over-all level
there should coexist a depressed level for the agricultural
components and an offsetting high level for the industrial
items. What then? Would not the American supported
program for farm products be adversely affected? No, it
would not be affected by any element of the commodity-
reserve mechanism. If world agricultural prices are low
under this plan it would be because farm products have
been greatly overproduced as against other products. If
that were so, world farm prices would be low in any case—
and they would probably be lower without a commodity-
reserve plan because there would then be no over-all support
mechanism in operation.[18]

It should be clear that the policy of supporting American
farm prices can only be helped by a sound policy on world
prices. The same is basically true of any other national
program looking toward stability and insulation from
external shocks of the economy. The British fear an international gold standard mainly because it would rapidly
transmit deflation from the United States to other nations.
A plan to stabilize the key raw materials is itself a potent
weapon against deflation and depression. There could be
nothing in such an arrangement that could possibly run
counter to the desire of any one country for stability and
balanced expansion.

As a final supposition let us assume that a nation preferred
not a stabilized price level but rather one that advanced
gradually in order to permit steadily rising wages and to
encourage business ventures.[19] Would a stable international
level interfere with such a policy? The answer is that it
would interfere no more than would a fluctuating world level.

If a nation wants to make its own price level it obviously
must insulate its prices from world prices. This it can do in
many different ways, e.g., (a) by means of tariffs, as tradition-

ally used in the United States; (*b*) by exchange depreciation, as was forced upon England in 1931; or (*c*) by a combination of internal and external fiscal policies, such as have been practiced by Sweden.[20] These measures may be effective or ineffective, praiseworthy or objectionable; the point is that there is nothing in the commodity-reserve concept which would make it more necessary than heretofore to resort to them or more difficult than heretofore to apply them successfully.

A Possible Role of Fabricated Merchandise as International Collateral

The trend of our reasoning leads us to offer a concrete suggestion for the *credit* operations of the IMF which will bring these also into closer harmony with the new emphasis on production and goods rather than on currency and banking entries. We would propose that, to the greatest extent feasible, claims against debtor nations be invested promptly in staple merchandise purchased within such nations. Such merchandise would consist, typically, not of raw materials but of standard grades of fabricated goods. For convenience, these operations might be carried on by a subsidiary of the IMF—say, "Staple Goods Corporation."

The effect of these purchases would be similar to a corresponding amount of exports by the debtor country, and they would accordingly wipe out its obligation to the IMF. They would thus realize immediately the Keynesian objective of ultimately balancing accounts through purchase of goods by credit-balance nations. In the same way as by such buying, they would create a demand for the products of the basic manufacturing industries of the debtor country and thus stimulate employment and general prosperity therein. Instead of entering competitive channels of trade in the creditor countries—for which their markets are not at once prepared—the merchandise would be held at an intermediate, noncompetitive point, where it would still function as a tangible asset of the IMF.

Both the White plan[21] and the Keynes plan[22] provided that collateral may be required from countries owing too much money on international account. Good collateral improves the security of an international debt, but the problem of enforcing payment remains a thorny one.[23] The transformation of claims held by the IMF into merchandise within the owing country may appear to involve a host of administrative complications. These should not be minimized, but it is almost certain that ownership of goods in the form suggested will yield better results to credit-balance countries than will ownership of book claims or foreign currencies.

The goods-investment device supplies an extremely valuable criterion of eligibility for international credit. If the subsidiary agency can readily acquire staple merchandise in the debtor country, this will mean that country holds liquid resources or productive capacity entitling it to credits of corresponding magnitude. If the country has no staple goods to spare and cannot produce them against order, it may well have a valid claim for relief but not for banking-type accommodation.

The liquidation of the merchandise held by the Staple Goods Corporation could take place under whatever conditions would have permitted the import-balance countries to pay off their borrowings. In effect the corporation will have substituted itself both on the books of the IMF and in the world export markets for the debtor nations. To the extent that *other goods* are sold abroad in their place—generating the needed foreign exchange—the goods held by the corporation can be disposed of *within* the debtor country. Where the credits would have been repaid rapidly in due course, there is obviously no net advantage in the merchandise-investment program. Where payment would otherwise have been doubtful or improperly withheld, the ownership of the merchandise should constitute a prime advantage to the credit agency.

The proposed purchasing of staple goods would constitute an application within a restricted field of the underlying idea of commodity-reserve currency. Fabricated merchandise of standard grades has sound economic value, but it may not lend itself to the generalized commodity-reserve treatment. Subject to the limitations to be imposed on the amount of advances by the IMF, such buying of useful goods could be made to contribute to a sound world economy at three points: (*a*) by expanding production and later consumption of things we need, (*b*) by stimulating trade and employment in the nations making the goods, and (*c*) by providing a physical backing for the credits granted in the process of stabilizing international exchange rates.

This final suggestion, however, is to be taken, not as an integral portion of the commodity-unit plan, but as a tentative effort to extend its philosophy into a related field.

Chapter X

COMMODITY-UNIT STABILIZATION AND OTHER ECONOMIC THINKING

> "If we fix our minds upon the fact that the capacity to produce is the nation's wealth, and upon the dislocation of that capacity as the supreme evil to be avoided, we shall, I believe, have hold of the saving truth."
>
> —WALTER LIPPMANN, *New York Herald Tribune*, Jan. 8, 1944.

IN this concluding chapter we shall attempt to relate our proposals to the main currents of economic thought for the postwar world. This examination may be carried on in two different areas. The first is that of alternative or complementary plans; the second is that of mental attitudes. We should begin, obviously, with our own field, and inquire what schemes or ideas having to do with basic raw materials are now competing for public attention.

Under the heading of objectives there are four in the commodities field which have been given prominence. These are (*a*) equal access to raw materials, (*b*) expansion of production, (*c*) stabilization of the price level, and (*d*) protection through stockpiles. In more general economic thinking the chief emphasis is constantly laid upon the necessity of high-level employment, but this is largely equivalent to the aim of expanding production. The first objective is mentioned in the Atlantic Charter, the second in the Lend-Lease Agreements, the third in the American and British currency proposals, and the fourth in a number of writings and in pending legislation.[1] There appears to be no important difference of opinion regarding the desirability of these aims, with the exception of some doubt—which the writer shares—as to the concrete meaning of the phrase "equal access to raw materials." Perhaps the most satisfactory definition of the phrase is the official pronouncement in May, 1942, of Sumner Welles (then Under Secretary of State): "Access means the right to buy in peaceful trade and it exists wherever that right is peaceful and secure."[2]

Our proposal for stabilizing the value of a raw-materials unit is unquestionably consonant with the objectives just listed. At least it should make access to basic commodities easier for all countries, since there will be an international stock to draw upon and since a nation's raw products can then more readily be turned into general purchasing power. It will provide at the same time the strongest incentive for a balanced expansion of production—an unfailing market— and an automatic mechanism for stabilizing the value of the commodity group. It will facilitate the possession by the United States and other countries of stockpiles of raw materials of much larger dimensions than are practicable under the commercial inventory method.

What other plans have been offered directed toward the same objectives? It seems fair to say that the alternative proposals are few, and these are either less definite or less comprehensive than the one herein suggested. The most concrete and clear-cut scheme is undoubtedly that for price stabilization of individual products by means of international commodity agreements—the advantages and limitations of which we have discussed in detail in Chap. IV. Beyond this we have seen many references to an "International Commodity Corporation,"—which will presumably buy, stockpile, and sell—but no complete account of its organization or operations has been given.[3] Congress has before it the Scrugham Bill providing for the purchase and stockpiling by the Government of various strategic metals. There appear to be plans under consideration by our State Department for accepting and stockpiling raw materials in exchange for our exports of manufactured goods;[4] and also the somewhat shadowy project for a "World Cartel" to control production, markets, and possibly prices.[5]

Thus, to bring about reasonable price stability in world commodities we appear to have our choice of two broad techniques, embracing five concrete alternatives. These are:

A. The control or cartel technique
    1. International Commodity Agreements with their probable emphasis upon stability at the expense of production.
    2. An International Commodity Control Board with powers to regiment producers everywhere.
B. The free production and stockpile technique
    3. National stockpiling of favored products, *e.g.*, metals, by special legislation.
    4. An International Commodity (purchase and sale) Corporation operating in separate products—with its almost inevitable tendency to load itself with commodities in weak position, and thus to move ultimately in the direction of controls and cartelization.
    5. An International Agency operating by the commodity-unit method and thus arriving at both over-all expansion and over-all stability, but reserving exceptional treatment for those few overabundant materials which would still constitute a world problem even in the face of global prosperity.

Apart from the above, we can make individual arrangements, not closely related to price stabilization, for stockpiling certain strategic materials.

Turning now from the area of raw materials planning, let us ask what other economic proposals are prominently before the world. Reviewing this question in February, 1943, the Commission to Study the Organization of Peace enumerated five or six separate economic functions and agencies contained in "suggestions deserving of serious study." These are: A Relief and Rehabilitation Authority (now established as UNNRA); a United Nations Shipping Administration, along with an organization "for controlling transit or power in various areas"; a United Nations Monetary Authority (since elaborated into the projected International Monetary Fund); a Commodity Corporation;[6] a United Nations Development Authority (now embodied in the proposed Bank for Reconstruction and Development).[7]

The sponsors of the noncommodity measures in no wise imply that their adoption will make planning for raw materials unnecessary. On the contrary, many of their statements call specifically for a separate and complementary technique to stabilize commodities.[8] There should be no conflict of aims or opinion, therefore, between those economists interested chiefly in financial rehabilitation and those addressing themselves more directly to the structure of world production. It is true that our own scheme has an important monetary aspect, in that we suggest that the commodity units can qualify as the backing for international currency. Perhaps we are here trespassing on monetary preserves; we hope, rather, that we are bringing aid from the commodity field to those struggling with the problem of constituting a sound and adequate currency for the modern world.

It must be admitted that the foregoing analysis oversimplifies the question we raised at the outset—*viz.*, the relation of our proposal to other plans and other economic thinking. The attitude of economists toward new proposals is conditioned very largely by the school of thought to which they belong, and—if they, too, are pioneers—by a natural bias in favor of their own program. Laymen also are not without prejudices in this field; and even the thoughtful and unbiased among them are necessarily influenced by a double mistrust—of their own untutored judgment and of economic innovations in general. Thus they turn for guidance to the experts; but among these is to be found neither unity of opinion or approach, nor even a well-defined weight of authority. It is a misfortune of the times that all of us must needs be amateur economists—including, and perhaps especially, the professionals.

The writer, like others, is subject to these disabilities. He must warn any unwary readers that his words have no established and authoritative doctrine behind them, and his most objective judgments are not without their leavening of prejudice. This caveat uttered, it may be illuminating to discuss the reception hitherto accorded the commodity-reserve idea. As a plan for the United States alone, it has been before American critics for more than 10 years, and in comprehensive form since 1937.[9]

During this period there has accumulated a fairish volume of comment by economists. Subject to correction, it seems in order to observe that the favorable appraisals have largely outweighed the hostile ones. Either sympathetic treatment or outright endorsement has been accorded the proposal by Professors Johnson of Yale and the New School,[10] Graham of Princeton,[11] King of New York University,[12] Lester of Duke,[13] Agger of Rutgers,[14] Reed of Cornell,[15] etc. More recently, F. A. Hayek of the London School of Economics has given the plan his strong support in its international application.[16]

Published unfavorable analyses have not been many. The most comprehensive is a "Critique of Commodity-Reserve Currency," by Messrs. Beale, Kennedy, and Winn of the University of Pennsylvania, published in the *Journal of Economics* in December, 1942. Professor Hayek's article in the (British) *Economic Journal* was followed by a comment by Lord Keynes, which naturally attracted wide attention. This paper appeared to reject the objective of a stable price level, on the grounds—it would seem—that steadily rising prices are necessary to maintain full employment. For the reader's enlightenment both the "Critique" and Lord Keynes's comment are reprinted in Appendix IV, together with replies by the present author.[17]

The criticisms, and the answers thereto, set forth at the end of this book should supply at least a fair outline of the connected arguments pro and contra.[18] Beyond these there is the climate of economic opinion, which controls the reception accorded an idea more powerfully than any extended critique. Since our proposal has several facets, the reactions to it tend to be fragmentary rather than integrated. For example, the commodity reserve idea has been viewed, variously, as (*a*) a method of establishing stockpiles, (*b*) a method of stabilizing the price level, (*c*) as a monetary or purchasing-power measure, and (*d*) as a method of stimulating production and employment. Under each heading the attitudes encountered may be of interest.

A. The Stockpiling Aspect

There is no school of thought which is opposed to the stockpile principle on a logical basis. For reasons explained in Chap. III there is an ingrained fear among businessmen of large inventories, and they have already become nervous about the results of the large governmental accumulations of materials. There is undoubtedly a sincere willingness on the part of businessmen to accept a comprehensive stockpiling policy, *provided* they could feel sure that these would be held for emergency needs only and would not overhang the commercial markets. This viewpoint has been eloquently espoused by Wm. L. Batt, and it is summarized also in the following remark of Dr. H. F. Grady, head of the American President Lines: "The stockpile principle is now fully accepted by this country though it was opposed for many years."[19]

It is true, of course, that vehement anti-New Dealers reject the ever-normal granary concept *in toto* as an idealistic impracticability. Typical of this attitude is the following squib from the financial page of a New York newspaper: "Experience is a poor teacher when the pupil is a bit dumb. It is now reported that one of those blueprints drawn at the International Food conference provides for an 'ever-normal' supply of food for the World."[20]

More temperate critics have expressed doubts as to the efficacy of the stockpile device as the resolver of great problems all by itself. This was the view of the French group of delegates at the Hot Springs Conference. The student's attitude on this subject is likely to be influenced greatly by the particular type of stockpile proposal he is considering. For example, the thorough examination of the "New International Wheat Agreements" made by Joseph S. Davis, to which we have already referred, contains a long section devoted to the reserve stock provisions in this compact.[21] He considers the stocks therein projected to be burdensome, and therefore too large; but his reasons are related to the particular machinery which requires each exporting country to make its own arrangements to carry its surplus. At the end of his critique occurs this significant passage:

> If an equalization reserve of wheat stocks is desirable with a view to narrowing the range of fluctuations in international wheat prices over a period of years, such reserves might better be held by an international nonpolitical corporation, under conditions so wisely determined and so widely understood that they could be taken fully into account by all interests concerned and would lessen trading risks rather than increase them.[22]

We submit that the commodity-unit proposal would meet the requirements stated by Dr. Davis. It is doubtful whether that would be true of an ICC operating in single products at the discretion of its managers.

Of the many stockpiling suggestions that have been made to date some provide a national and others an international technique.[23] These two approaches are not in conflict. Since an international reserve must be held somewhere, it can be physically apportioned and thus made equivalent to a number of national reserves. Our proposal provides for this. In addition, there would be no obstacle to the acquisition of supplementary reserves by a nation acting only for itself.

B. The Matter of Price Stability

In this area we encounter various shades of opinion. There is some orthodox opposition to price stability on the ground that prices should decline secularly with technical improvements.[24] There has also been voiced—perhaps a somewhat token—hostility to stabilization as a possible step towards stagnation.[25] Quite contrary is the apparent view of Lord

Keynes, already referred to, that steadily rising prices may be required to maintain full employment. Still, whatever preference may be expressed as to long-term prices, there is a completely unanimous desire to eliminate the wide short-term fluctuations in raw-material prices that have devastated our economy.[26] Making due allowance for the weight of Lord Keynes' great authority, it is difficult for us to imagine a wide rejection by either economists or laymen of the simple idea that a paper dollar should always have the same value in terms of basic commodities as a group.

This very idea of stabilizing only the group value has failed to satisfy those who prefer the fixing of "just prices" for each commodity. This would include a minority of economists and a majority of our farm leaders. The farm organizations have not paid serious attention to our proposal, although it promises them an unlimited market at a stabilized over-all price for balanced production of their crops. Why? Apparently because a given farmer is interested in the price of wheat, or the price of cotton, rather than in farm prices generally. Apparently, also, because farmers have been reasonably successful in obtaining their heart's desire of parity prices for each separate crop, through the exertion of strong political pressures.

These reasons are not as good as they look. The alternative of over-all price stability for agriculture at a fair level is almost certain to work out in the long run so as to bring a fair average price for the major *individual* crops. More important, these prices will be obtained on larger production, because the emphasis can be placed on balanced expansion rather than on acreage restriction. Again, political victories gained by the farmers are double-edged. They create hostility and counterblocks. Most important of all, the farmer's price structure since 1933 has been won at the cost of a degree of regimentation which he is unlikely ever to accept with good grace. Hence the very policy he has favored arouses repugnance in his own mind as well as all about him. Henry A. Wallace, then Secretary of Agriculture, recognized this fact frankly in his pamphlet, *America Must Choose:*[27] "The farmer dislikes production control instinctively. He does not like to see land idle and people hungry. . . . Practically the entire population dislikes our basic program of controlling farm production." (p. 1.)

Perhaps one of the advantages of planning balanced expansion on the international rather than the national level is that the issues can there be viewed in a wider and more philosophical frame. If our statement of the farmer's true interest is a correct one, it is to be hoped that our influential farm organizations will choose carefully and well between the opposite principles of cartelization or "free coinage" of agricultural output.

C. The Monetary Aspect

One of the central elements in our proposal is that a commodity composite (though not the separate components) shall have the monetary status of gold, and thus function as the equivalent of an additional world currency. This mechanism is by no means *indispensable* to any international plan for stabilizing the price level of basic raw materials as a group. Conceivably, the composite units may be bought and sold, as proposed, but instead of their being self-financing, their cost may be defrayed by credit advances to the buying agency. This is the method of operating in *individual* commodities that most economists have envisaged,[28] and it could be applied just as well to composite purchases and sales.

We have introduced the monetary factor not by necessity but by choice. Its advantages are obvious. Self-financed commodity units are not only interest free, but free also from dependence upon credit conditions. They are a step—desirable, it seems to us—in the direction of a goods economy as distinct from a money economy; but this step is taken without violence by merely identifying basic goods with money. It guarantees unfailing purchasing power where it is most needed—among the countless producers of raw commodities. At the same time it improves the character of the world's money by putting behind it things universally usable and universally needed.

The proponent of this idea may have thought he had an ideal solution for some of our major difficulties, and that consequently he would be hailed as a benefactor of humanity. The welcome hitherto accorded his scheme has fallen measurably short of such acclaim. It has had some ardent supporters, to be sure, and the number appears to be increasing with dignified slowness. The large body of economists have preferred to maintain a discreet and silent neutrality. This must be on the grounds either that the subject is not important enough to warrant their attention—which can hardly be true—or more plausibly that the odds are so strongly against any novel proposal's having merit that it hardly pays to examine this one with any care.

This attitude displays the familiar contrast between the economists' insistence upon the necessity of a new approach in general and his instinctive resistance to any specific innovation. No doubt they will subscribe cheerfully to the remark of our Under Secretary of Commerce that "new financial concepts that will fit and serve economies of full production and maximum national income are in the making."[29] But that eager and open-minded curiosity, which is so sorely needed to winnow the grain from the chaff in monetary proposals, is still far from being a conspicuous attribute of our professional economists.

Those who have rejected the monetary aspects of our plan, after more or less thorough study, appear to fall into two opposite camps. On the one side are the orthodox gold-standard advocates. To them, as the elder Morgan said to the Pujo Committee in 1911, "the only true money is gold." Hence, commodity-backed money must be, by definition, heretical money. It is a newfangled unsoundness added to the oldfangled errors of silver money, fiat money, and managed money. These are matters of their religious belief and admit of no discussion—certainly of no useful discussion.

If the American gold-standardites were a little less intransigent in their attitude they might recognize that commodity-reserve currency is *their* kind of currency. It is hard money backed by full value. For better or worse, it is entirely unmanaged—save in minor details. These points have been well understood and made abundantly clear by Professor F. A. Hayek, one of the world's leading gold-standard advocates.[30]

As bearing on the psychology of gold-standard advocates, it is interesting to consider Professor E. W. Kemmerer's little pamphlet, entitled "High Spots in the Case for a Return to the International Gold Standard."[31] Early in his presentation he quotes the following from the famous "Report on Finance and Industry" made by the Macmillan Committee in 1931: "But there can be little or no hope of progress at an early date for the monetary system of the world, except as the result of a process of evolution, starting from the historic gold standard."[32] To which Kemmerer adds: "With this declaration I am in full agreement, and this article is a brief statement of my principal reasons for this judgment." He then proceeds to state the well-known advantages of the gold standard arising from (*a*) public confidence in it, (*b*) its automatic operation, (*c*) its international acceptance, and (*d*) the stability of gold's value.

Nothing is said in his pamphlet about the possibility of a "process of evolution starting from the historic gold standard." Yet this idea of *evolution* may well be the central idea of the statement quoted, with which Kemmerer places himself in full agreement. What could be a more logical process of evolution than the addition to gold of other commodities with much greater utility, while retaining the automatic mechanism and the concept of tangible and stable values behind currency? This is the essence of the commodity-unit proposal.

Gold-standard supporters should also realize that commodity-reserve currency is not a further threat to the already severely impaired monetary position of gold,[33] but rather a means of creating those conditions of economic stability which are essential to the smooth working of an international gold standard. The two currencies can exist side by side, just as gold certificates and silver certificates co-existed comfortably "in the good old days."

The technique of setting up a "composite equivalent" for a national currency has recently been given its first practical formulation. This appears in the reorganization of the monetary system of Paraguay, the details of which are presented in the *Federal Reserve Bulletin* for January, 1944.

The official announcement states that the value of the new Paraguayan unit, the *guaraní*, shall be determined by application of a "composite exchange standard." The technique is not worked out in detail, but it is implied that the value of the guaraní might be kept equivalent to the sum of appropriate components based on foreign currencies important in Paraguay's foreign trade. Let us give our own illustration of the possible mechanics of this composite standard. Assume that the foreign currencies taken are the American dollar, the British pound, and the Argentine peso; assume also that the relative weights are to be derived from the total trade with the three countries in a year such as 1937. The resultant equation of value would then work out somewhat as follows: One guaraní equals $0.07 plus 4*d* plus ¾ Argentine peso.

The similarity in form between the new "composite exchange standard" of Paraguay and our proposed composite commodity-unit standard for international money is evident. While the analogy should not be pressed too far, it is of interest as indicating that the principle of symmetallism has both practicability and a certain versatility in its application to the problems of modern currency.

Support for the general idea of using raw materials as a backing for money has come from various sources not considered to be crackpot or radical. Herbert Hoover and Hugh Gibson touch on this point—a bit cryptically, but nonetheless suggestively—in "Problems of Lasting Peace," in the following words:

Solution of the credit problem will have to be found through some sort of credit pool in which all nations pledge their resources. In this problem it will be necessary to examine the possibility of using a reserve of raw

materials to be created in time of lower prices and depressions as an
adjunct to international credit and currency stabilization.[34]

Dr. Paul Einzig, the prominent British economist, is more
explicit in his endorsement of the concept. He wrote: "The
admission of the principle that non-perishable staple commodities can be included in currency reserves to a limited
extent, we believe, would go a long way toward solving the
world's monetary problems, and also the present problem
of surplus stocks."[35]

It is worth pointing out that as the progress of war has
undermined currency values in many lands, there has been
a widespread resort to commodities for use as money. In
France and Belgium the land tax is payable not in money
but in ferrous metals, *i.e.*, copper scrap or the equivalent in
lead, zinc, etc.[36] In Shensi Province, China, wheat and flour
have replaced currency as a yardstick of value and for the
payment of taxes, salaries, and rents.[37] In January, 1944,
Hungary floated a 3 per cent wheat loan, in which payments
of both capital and interest will be determined by the price
of wheat.[38] Similarly there has been discussion in Italy of
the issuance of "State loans, not in lire or gold, but in coal
or rye, or evaluated according to an index compiled to show
the fluctuations in the true cost of living."[39]

A similar note was struck by the Brazilian Economic
Congress, held toward the end of 1943. It apparently rejected both the White and the Keynes proposals; instead, it
approved a suggestion calling for a "Bank of the American
Nations, which would issue money based not on the gold
standard but on production."[40]

The other camp opposed to commodity-reserve currency
consists of those who favor an unsecured, managed money.
They believe, in general, that the State should create and
supply whatever amount of currency is needed to keep
production and consumption functioning at a maximum
rate. If the supply becomes excessive, as shown by a
tendency of prices to rise, the mischievous portion should
be retired—presumably through taxation.[41] There is surely

nothing wrong with these objectives; the big question is whether money management will accomplish them. We share the doubts of conservative economists on this score. To our thinking, the relationship between currency emissions and withdrawals on the one side, and business activity and the price level on the other, is too indirect and unpredictable to promise good success from the management technique.

It is not easy to see why advocates of managed money should be strongly opposed to commodity-reserve currency. The latter mechanism aims, as they do, toward maintaining stable prices and maximum production. Money backed by materials must be at least as good inherently as unsecured currency; and if it will do the job that the management school wants done, it should clearly be preferred as less subject to abuse. A number of American economists with leanings toward managed money have realized this truth and have given their support to the commodity-reserve proposal.[42] Many, however, reject any and all backing for currency as "unnecessary," and commodity-unit backing in particular as "too complicated." It is for the reader to judge whether they are right.

D. *The Full Employment Aspect*

We do not assert that our plan to stockpile and stabilize raw materials will guarantee full employment. We do say that it will contribute greatly toward that end by expanding the output of primary commodities and by increasing the purchasing power of numerous small producers. Since it will eliminate wide fluctuations in prices it will narrow the swings of the business cycle, and thus reduce unemployment caused by cyclical depressions. On this point J. B. Condliffe's statement is most emphatic: "Only by concerted effort to avoid violent price fluctuations while carrying through necessary adjustments to the new postwar situation, can full employment be maintained."[43]

These are results of great value in themselves. Nevertheless, the proposal has been criticized because it will not assure every worker a job, and more particularly because it will not solve the vexing problems resulting from the uneven demand for capital goods. It is hardly fair to ask one proposal to cure all the economic ills of the world, and we make no pretension to do so. We do believe that price stability and narrower business cycles will be of considerable help to the capital goods producers, and also that the field is open for other plans to assist them further.[44]

All economists believe that the proper timing of public works would be a valuable means of counteracting booms and depressions. Many go much farther and insist that by proper management of a public works program the State can both create and maintain high-level employment. On this point there is a deep gulf between those who believe that deficit spending will prime the pump and bring a multiplied volume of other business activity in its train, and those who insist that this policy does much more damage through undermining investors' confidence than it does good by increasing purchasing power.[45]

Our proposal is neither pro-spending nor anti-spending, and it is unnecessary for us to take sides in this controversy. We do feel that the need for, or the excuse for, deficit spending would be measurably reduced or even eliminated through the expansionist effect of increased production and sale of agricultural and industrial raw materials under our plan. There is evident, however, a definite tendency on the part of economists of the "fiscal policy" school to view our ideas with a somewhat jaundiced eye. Their argument seems to be that public works or "selective expenditure" will stabilize prices and employment more effectively than a commodity reservoir mechanism.[46] It is difficult to understand this single reliance upon fiscal policy as the cure of all our major economic evils—especially in view of the time lag of tax measures, the question of the amount and selection of public works, the indirect and delayed relationship of government spending to the price level, the adverse psychological effects of continued deficits, etc.

To us it appears that advocates of control measures through fiscal policy should welcome as auxiliaries to their program all supplementary mechanisms which would narrow the cyclical fluctuations that they must wrestle with and which would reduce the area for the exercise of discretionary and hazardous economic management.

CONCLUSION

The foregoing discussion has sought to point out the schools and shades of economic opinion among which our proposal must make its way. Since we have touched upon many facets it might be natural for the reader to conclude that our plan is not only ambitious but complicated or cumbersome as well. The latter, we think, is not so. One must distinguish between the implications of an idea, which may be many-sided and far-reaching, and the idea itself, which may be essentially simple. In "Storage and Stability" we summarized the terms of our plan in a single sentence: "It proposes to accord to a composite group of basic commodities exactly the same monetary status as was formerly given to gold."[47] In its present international version we suggest, quite tentatively, that buying and selling points be set at 95 per cent and 105 per cent, respectively, of the standard value of the unit. We also suggest that international commodity agreements, in their more enlightened forms, be employed as an adjunct in the case of products which are in an especially weak position.

This is hardly a complex proposal.[48] There are, of course, substantial technical difficulties in establishing an appropriate commodity unit, but these are of a character that analysts have dealt with successfully for many years. In one respect the commodity-unit approach should measurably simplify the problem of stabilizing raw materials. It reduces to one issue what would otherwise be a dozen or more separate fields of dispute relating to the proper price and allocation policies for individual commodities. In the single area of the commodity unit the pernicious practice of logrolling will more readily be replaced by a reasonably scientific technique for establishing the relative quantitative importance of the several commodities.[49]

An interesting analogy may be drawn between the apportionment of commodity weights in the unit and the allocation of federal highway funds among the 48 states. Here, too, we have a goodly number of claimants for the most generous treatment possible. Yet a comparatively simple formula has been worked out, which has been subject to a minimum of political wrangling.[50]

Contrast the businesslike process of allocating highway or education funds with the scandalous influence of pressure groups in fixing tariff rates. The same distinction holds in the commodity field. If each is to be assisted independently of all others, the result is certain to be limitless demands and clamorous confusion. If they are drawn together into a carefully constructed commodity unit, then any unreasonable demand can succeed only at the expense of all other affected producers, and it is likely to make little headway.

There is one guiding economic principle for the future that has been subscribed to by all the conferences and all the great pronouncements. It is "that the world, after the war, should follow a bold policy of economic expansion instead of the timid regime of scarcity which characterized the 1930's."[51]

We believe it merely a statement of fact to assert that the plan developed herein is the only concrete and comprehensive suggestion submitted to date for carrying out this principle—the only one which undertakes directly to encourage a balanced expansion of the production of basic raw materials throughout the world.

Our great danger is that we shall pay lip service to the ideal of abundance, but to preserve needed stability, we shall follow the devious paths of cartelized restriction. To avoid this lame and impotent conclusion, we must promote expansion not by brave words but by direct and practicable techniques.

CHAPTER NOTES

Chapter I

1. See *Report of the Committee for the Study of Raw Materials*, Series of League of Nations Publications, 1937, II.B.7; *Report on Certain Aspects of the Raw Materials Problem*, League of Nations Document C.51, M. 18. 1922; E. Dennery, rapporteur, *Le Problème des matières premières*, Institut International de Cooperation Intellectuelle, Société des Nations, Paris, 1939.

2. Per capita figures on coffee consumption of various nations are given in V. O. Wickizer, *The World Coffee Economy*, Food Research Institute, Stanford University, August, 1943, p. 14.

3. This was the chief conclusion reached by Prof. C. Gini in his *Report on the Problem of Raw Materials*, made to the League of Nations in 1931, League of Nations Publication 8.

4. A. P. Lerner's article, "Functional Finance and the Federal Debt," in *Social Research*, New York, February, 1943, pp. 38*ff*., presents the case for expanding the national debt to any extent needed without limits or fear. More moderate expositions of the "compensatory spending" doctrine are found in Stuart Chase's, *Where's the Money Coming From?*, New York, 1943; and Robert R. Nathan's *Mobilizing for Abundance*, New York, 1944. The conservative viewpoint in rebuttal appears in the *Monthly Letters of The National City Bank of New York*, December, 1943, pp. 139–43 and January, 1944, pp. 7–11; also in Alfred Kähler, "The Public Debt in the Financial Structure," *Social Research*, February, 1944, pp. 11–26.

5. References to the particularly vulnerable position of such countries are frequent in the utterances of both economists and businessmen. The fact that "the primary producing countries" were the first to be forced off the gold standard in the depression of the 1930's is pointed out by the U.S. Department of Commerce, *The U.S. in the World Economy*, 1943, p. 6. The notable pamphlet of Lever Bros. on "The Problem of Unemployment," London, 1943, p. 22, states: "The vicissitudes of raw materials producing countries have played an important part in the creation of booms and depressions." The following is typical of League of Nations' statements on this point: "A reasonable degree of stability in the prices of raw materials is of the greatest importance to countries whose exports mainly take that form, as their economy cannot function normally in the presence of violent changes in values of the exports on which they

principally rely for their supplies of foreign currencies." (Report of the Financial Committee: "Some Observations on the General Situation," Geneva, 1938.)

6. *Daily Index No. of Basic Commodities Prices*, published by U.S. Bureau of Labor Statistics, using August, 1939, as 100.

7. *Cf.* on this point the writer's address, "Inflation Prospects and Investment Policy," published in *Commercial and Financial Chronicle*, Dec. 21, 1943, p. 1.

8. Address to the American Management Association, reported in *The New York Times*, Jan. 14, 1944. A similarly pessimistic forecast with respect to the postwar position of the American farmer, unless new price support programs are undertaken, was made in a report on "Problems of Agricultural Policy after the War," presented by T. W. Schultz to the Agricultural Committee of the National Planning Association in early 1944. (See Supplement to that body's *Public Policy Digest*, March, 1944, p. 2.)

9. *After the War*—1919–1920, National Resources Planning Board, June, 1943, p. 45.

10. *Commercial Policy in the Interwar Period*, League of Nations, 1942.

11. *The Economist*, London, Dec. 4, 1943, p. 751.

Chapter II

1. "Report on Postwar Economic Policy and Planning," *Senate Document* 106, Oct. 12, 1943, p. 22.

2. "United States—United Kingdom Lend-lease Agreement," Art. VI.

3. J. Anton De Haas, "Economic Peace through Private Agreements," *Harvard Business Review*, Winter, 1944, p. 149.

4. All but six of the states have passed these price-maintenance, or "fair-trade," laws. However, the U.S. Department of Justice insists that in some cases they have been used to effect collusive price fixing by manufacturers or distributors, and has instituted antitrust suits, *e.g.*, against national drug associations and liquor retailers. (See *Business Week*, Mar. 11, 1944, pp. 29, 34.)

5. *Cf.* the following from an editorial in *The Wall Street Journal*, Sept. 14, 1943: "It is hard to imagine a concert of nations undertaking to raise the world's living standards without also undertaking to reverse this world-wide trend toward the cartelization of the farmer."

6. The 1937 *Report of Committee for the Study of the Problems of Raw Materials* draws "a clear distinction" between governmental and private schemes of control, favoring the former for the reasons here stated. (*Op. cit.*, p. 17.)

7. Sir Edgar Jones is head of the British Steel Cartel. A similar program has been advanced by Lord MacGowan, head of Imperial Chemical Industries. See Part Two of *The New Republic*, Mar. 27, 1944, entitled

"Cartels"; it contains much information and a vigorous attack on the entire cartel movement.

8. *Cf.* in particular the article, "Restraint of Trade," in *The Economist*, London, June 6, 1942, pp. 781–782. Discussing reports on reconstruction by three large business bodies, it says, "There is the paradox. On the one hand these documents make a notable plea for freedom and expansion. On the other hand they paint a picture of control, restraint, and restriction, both at home and abroad, a picture of national and international autarky and of self-rule by vested interests." Sir William Beveridge has also called attention to the tendency of British business "towards limitation or suppression of competition by agreement between individual producers, opening the door both to inefficiency and to exploitation." (See article on "The Purpose of Industry," in *The Times*, London, June 28, 1943, p. 7.) Criticisms of this kind antedate the war, as shown by the statement in *Spectator*, Mar. 3, 1939: " . . . there are many signs that British leaders are coming to think in terms of national development by controlled monopolies." (Quoted by F. A. Hayek in his article, "Planning, Science, and Freedom," in *Nature*, Nov. 15, 1941.)

9. *Cf.* the advice to business given in *Second Report of the Postwar Committee of the National Association of Manufacturers*, December, 1941: "Be competitive; avoid all forms of agreements or understandings with competitors which restrict production or distribution or attempt to establish prices."

The Standard Oil Company of New Jersey, one of the centers of the cartel controversy, has this to say about its position: "As explained in public statements, the management of your company opposes the cartel method of doing business. It is not, however, in a position to force its views upon the governments or the nationals of whatever countries may favor or require that method. If we are to do business in foreign countries we must observe their laws and customs." (Proxy Statement, Apr. 27, 1944, p. 10.)

10. His viewpoint is summarized in the following sentence: "No American can intelligently and sincerely promise you any cooperation in any system of world-wide cartels, for the average American would call it economic imperialism, and he is against it." (Speech to the Association of British Chambers of Commerce, Aug. 18, 1943.) Note also his statement to *The Christian Science Monitor*, on his return from England: "Whereas businessmen in the United States work under the profit and loss system of free enterprise and competition, the British are very desirous of a guarantee and no losses through the use of cartels and monopolies." (Sept. 3, 1943, p. 14.)

11. An article in the *Wall Street Journal*, Jan. 31, 1944, p. 4, lists 16 "international cartel suits" as currently pending. It states further that the Department of Justice has a list of 179 cartel agreements in force in

1939, American enterprises being involved in 109 of these. The great bulk of the cartels covered manufactured goods. The study entitled "Economic and Political Aspects of International Cartels" (*Monograph* 1, Senate Committee Printing, 78th Congress, 2d Session), gives various details relating to a large number of cartel operations, most of which have involved American firms.

12. The following press comment is typical on this point: "In the State Department there are all colors of opinion regarding cartels, the most 'official' being that complete eradication would be desirable, but that this is not practicable, and that the United States policy should, therefore, concentrate upon keeping them within bounds." (*Business Week*, Jan. 15, 1944, p. 15.)

13. Quoted from article, "World Cartel," in *The Wall Street Journal*, Jan. 13, 1944, pp. 1, 6. A more plausible account of the activities of the State Department appeared later, in *The Wall Street Journal* of Apr. 24, 1944. Here the proposal is presented as "the formation of a sort of world-wide federal trade commission to check cartels."

14. *Department of State Bulletin*, June 19, 1943.

15. The buffer-stock viewpoint was strongly supported in a statement published by the head of the British delegation, R. K. Law. The opposite viewpoint was taken publicly by the French delegation. (See *The New York Times*, May 24, 1943, p. 7.) There is a striking inversion of the positions of the United States and Great Britain when cartel discussion shifts from finished goods to raw materials. Note the following summary of the two viewpoints at the Food Conference, in *The New Republic*, June, 14, 1943, p. 786: "American planning aims to maintain a price considered fair to the producers, to limit production to the amount that can be sold at that price, and to allocate the international market among the various producing nations. The British, on the other hand, favor the idea of 'buffer stocks,' which would aim not at supporting any given price but at stabilizing the market as between good and bad years." This description of "American planning" for foodstuffs fits perfectly the *British* cartel idea for *finished goods*.

Chapter III

1. *Op. cit.* p. 63.

2. "Raw Materials: War and Post-war," in *State Department Bulletin*, Apr. 24, 1943, p. 342.

3. Address to American Finance Conference, Nov. 17, 1943.

4. See p. 28.

5. A dramatic instance of this fact is afforded by wheat. Troublesome surpluses of this commodity existed even three years after the outbreak of the Second World War. In July, 1942. An official document referred to "the present serious wheat-surplus problem in the four overseas exporting

countries," as the first fundamental reason for negotiating the International Wheat Agreement in that year. (See reference to this statement in J. S. Davis, *The New International Wheat Agreements*, Food Research Institute, Stanford University, November, 1942, p. 29.) In July, 1943, Argentina announced her intention of burning 75 million bushels of wheat for fuel because of the glut. (*The New York Times*, July, 25, 1943.)

Yet by January, 1944, the situation had changed completely, at least for the United States. Marvin Jones, War Food Administrator, issued a statement predicting "a critical shortage of wheat" in this country, unless imports from Canada could be arranged. (*Wall Street Journal*, Jan. 18, 1944.)

6. For references to restrictions on consumption of coal, meat, wheat, and sugar in the United States during the First World War, see this author's *Storage and Stability*, New York, 1937, p. 250.

7. Business inventories in the United States at the end of 1939 totaled nearly 20 billion dollars of which 10.7 billion were held by manufacturers, 3.5 billion by wholesalers, and 5.3 billion by retailers. (*Survey of Current Business*, March, 1944, p. 15.) These holdings were physically equivalent to about 40 billion dollars of merchandise at retail prices—perhaps five-sixths of the year's consumption of goods.

8. For numerous references to this practice, see *Storage and Stability* pp. 26–32.

9. *Cf. ibid.*, pp. 32, 241–242.

10. See for example, Mr. Batt's address before the Bond Club, New York City, Feb. 23, 1944.

11. *Business Week*, Dec. 11, 1943, pp. 42, 44. An elaborate account in *The Wall Street Journal*, Jan. 6, 1944, p. 1, ascribes this general proposal to the State Department.

12. For a discussion of the Ever-normal Granary provision of the Agricultural Adjustment Act of 1938, see *Storage and Stability*, pp. 183–188.

13. See article 3. "RFC War Loans Set at $11.5 Billion up to March 7," in *The Wall Street Journal*, Mar. 23, 1942, and "Mountain of Metal," *ibid.*, July 17, 1944, p. 1.

14. See article, "Wool Piles Up," in *Business Week*, Feb. 5, 1944, pp. 41–43; also article, "Smothered in Wool," in *The Wall Street Journal*, Apr. 24, 1944, p. 1. The problem was quite similar at the end of the First World War. *Cf. The Government and Wool*, 1917–1920, Agriculture History Series 6, U.S. Department of Agriculture, August, 1943.

15. *Cf.* article, "Metal Men Ponder Stockpile Program," in *The New York Times*, Dec. 12, 1943, 5:1.

16. *Newsweek*, Nov. 22, 1943, p. 18.

17. *The Times*, London.

18. Newer accounting techniques are reducing the business hazards resulting from year-to-year fluctuations in the quoted market values of

the same physical amount of inventory. These include "LIFO" (last-in-first-out), and the base-stock method. There remains, however, "the abhorrence of the existing economic system to large stocks of commodities"—a phrase ascribed to Keynes by Lord Melchett. (*Parliamentary Debates on an International Clearing Union*, British Information Services, New York, July, 1943, p. 86.)

19. Figures for whisky and tobacco inventories in relation to consumption are published monthly by *Survey of Current Business*. A reference to the lumber inventory situation appears on p. 74 of "Report on Economic Policy and Planning," *Senate Document* 104, Oct. 12, 1943. By taking green lumber out of the drying yards to meet the emergency needs of war we have managed to turn these yards into a sort of "ever-normal timbery."

20. This point is brought out in picturesque fashion by Flaubert's description of the sumptuary wealth amassed by Hamilcar Barca of Carthage. (*Salammbo*, Chap. V.)

The reluctance of modern wealth to take the form of merchandise presents not only a psychological contrast with earlier times but also an economic departure of great and troublesome significance. The buffer-stock or reservoir function of business inventories as a whole is seriously undermined by the fierce emphasis that business lays upon keeping its inventories down to the minimum. We should have a similar effect if the keepers of water reservoirs were chiefly concerned with keeping the water level as low as possible.

Cf. the following significant passage from the address of Lord Keynes on "The Policy of Government Storage of Foodstuffs and Raw Materials," in *The Economic Journal*, September, 1938: "It is an outstanding fault of the competitive system that there is no sufficient incentive to individual enterprise to store surplus stocks of materials so as to maintain continuity of output and to average, so far as possible, periods of high and low demand."

Chapter IV

1. The International Wheat Agreement provides that the United States, Canada, Argentina, and Australia shall "ensure that stocks of old wheat held at the end of their respective crop years" shall be within a specified range. The "standard minimum" aggregates 290 million bushels and the "standard maximum" 885 million bushels for the four exporting nations. (*New International Wheat Agreements, op cit.*, p. 49.)

2. See *op. cit.* Also "International Commodity Agreements in the Post-war World," *American Economic Review*, March, 1942, pp. 391–403; and paper with same title included in *Postwar Economic Problems*, New York, 1943, pp. 305–321.

3. E. Dennery, *op. cit.*, p. 94. Translation by this author. The reference included is to J. C. L. Rowe, *Markets and Men*, New York, 1936, pp. 166, 167.

4. *The Wall Street Journal*, Aug. 21, 1943, p. 1.

5. "Report on Reconstruction," published by British Chamber of Commerce, New York, 1942.

6. See editorial in *The Wall Street Journal*, May 27, 1943.

Chapter V

1. We might point out that the Beveridge *Report on Social Insurance and Allied Services* for Britain also used figures based on a cost of living 25 per cent above the 1938 figure, subject to adjustment for later changes. (Par. 27 of the *Report*, New York, 1942.)

2. An analogous arrangement has been in operation with respect to the United States government loans on corn which is stored on the borrower's farm. The government has supplied storage bins. An allowance for storage expense is made after ownership is taken over by the Commodity Credit Corporation.

3. See table in *Storage and Stability*, p. 275.

4. See *Storage and Stability*, pp. 98–104. This is referred to again, p. 81.

5. Quoted in *The Times*, London, Jan. 11, 1944, p. 7.

6. See *Report of Section II. Expansion of Production and Adaptation to Consumption Needs*, Department of State Publication 1948, Conference Series 52, Washington, 1943, pp. 52*ff.*

7. Participation in the International Wheat Agreement, when effective, will be open to the government of any country, acceding either as an importing or exporting country. (Art. XIV.) Each such government will have representation on the International Wheat Council, which will administer the agreement. However, details as to voting have not yet been worked out. (Art. VII, and Note.) The text of the agreement was published by the U.S. Department of Agriculture in July, 1942.

The Inter-American Coffee Board, administering the Coffee Agreement, has delegates from 15 countries. The United States delegate, representing consumers, is given 12 votes—one-third of the total. (J. B. Gibbs, "The Inter-American Coffee Agreement" in *Foreign Agriculture*, April, 1941, p. 168.)

8. Note that the destruction of coffee continued in Brazil even after adoption of the Coffee Agreement.

9. The same point is made by the proponents of international commodity agreements. See Chap. II, p. 18.

10. For a standard treatment of this subject, see J. Backman, "Government Control of Prices," in *Planned Society*, New York, 1937, Chapter XI.

11. Contemporary economists of the conservative school like to dilate upon the Edict of Diocletian (A.D. 301) as a harrowing example of price fixing run mad. This edict was without doubt overambitious; it dealt with results instead of causes, and its efforts to freeze all prices was doomed to

inevitable failure in the difficult conditions then confronting the Roman Empire. The modern critics content themselves with quoting the violent strictures written by Bishop Lactantius, an historian of the period. In so doing they may make insufficient allowance for the great animosity of Lactantius against Diocletian, based on religious grounds. Certainly they give us no hint of the high position accorded by history to that emperor as one of the ablest administrators of the Roman Empire. Gibbon, who wrote at length and on the whole admiringly of Diocletian, does not mention the edict and its consequences. Quite recently, Rebecca West has had some interesting things to say on this very point in her great work, *Black Lamb and Grey Falcon, e.g.:* "He (Diocletian) maintained the Empire in a state of apparent equilibrium for 21 years. The invasion of the barbarians was an immediate danger, but only because the Empire was so internally weakened by economic problems. Of these nobody knew the solution at the beginning of the fourth century, and indeed they have not been solved now in the middle of the twentieth century." (p. 146.)

Chapter VI

1. "World Institutions for Stability and Expansion," *Foreign Affairs*, January, 1944, pp. 248–258. J. B. Condliffe has a very similar description of the functions of a United Nations Commodity Corporation in his essay, "Problems of Economic Reorganization," published by the Committee to Study the Organization of Peace, January, 1943, p. 37.

2. Dean Acheson, quoted in *The New York Times*, May 25, 1944.

3. During 1943–1944 wartime scarcity conditions showed themselves in a persistent premium for spot deliveries over futures in the case of a number of commodities. Examples: At the end of May, 1944, such premiums existed in barley, cotton, oats, rye, wheat, wool tops, etc. See tables in *The Wall Street Journal*, June 1, 1944, p. 8.

A similar situation existed in 1936–1937, due to the combination of drought and commodity speculation. For details see the table in *Storage and Stability*, p. 278. Thus the proposed substitution technique could have yielded a substantial income to the commodity-unit reservoir on two important occasions in the past decade.

4. *Op. cit.*, p. 133.

5. Prof. T. W. Schultz has developed a somewhat similar idea as applied solely to agricultural products in the United States. He suggests that prices for each important farm product be fixed a year in advance so that the farmer can plan his crops in accordance with the best estimate of current agricultural needs. See *Redirecting Farm Policy*, New York, 1943.

6. *Free World*, September, 1943, contains an article by R. J. Scanlan, entitled "The Economic Reserve System," which advocates a plan quite

similar to that of Grondona. A mint price will be established for each major basic commodity, which will then be bought and sold by the government in unlimited quantities at that price. Once set, the mint price must be "long maintained, with no changes except after long advance notice" (p. 213). Large reserves are expected to be accumulated and to be financed by low-interest loans.

Scanlan suggests that National Economic Reserve Systems be established on a domestic basis for those commodities which are not exported, while an International Economic Reserve System could be later set up to apply to important products entering into world trade. He states there would be no conflict between the two systems as each "would cover different commodities, with no duplication." This aspect of the idea would appear rather questionable.

The *Free World* article was evidently intended as an introduction to Scanlan's plan; hence it contains a great deal more of general observation and advocacy than it does of detailed, technical exposition.

7. *Op. cit.*, pp. 89–93.

8. *Op. cit.*, p. 95.

9. At the end of Grondona's book occurs a passage strongly favoring the cartel system—so organized, of course, as "to ensure a reasonable return on exports from all manufacturing countries having European standards of living; while assuring supplies to 'poor' markets at prices the people in such countries are able to pay." He adds that "a wide expansion of the cartel system . . . sanely administered, would be a boon indeed."

Since there does not appear to be any organic connection between this fervent plea for cartels and Grondona's plan for dealing with commodities, I have not touched upon it in the body of the discussion. It may have relevant significance as indicating an underlying willingness on his part to accept the cartelization of certain *raw materials* if that should be needed to maintain their separately fixed prices.

10. *Op. cit.*, p. 13. In addition, Harrod believes that a composite plan will not apply the necessary correctives to speculative operations in individual, too volatile, commodities. (*Ibid.*, p. 13.) Under conditions of relative stability such speculation rarely gets far enough to cause serious harm. The provision by which individual commodities may be sold out of the units and replaced by futures contracts bought at a discount will provide an important practical check upon speculation for the rise.

11. *Report of the Royal Gold and Silver Commission*, 1888, pp. 126–127.

12. This significant phrase was used by Alfred P. Sloan, Jr., president of General Motors Corporation, in his address before the Second War Congress of the National Manufacturers Association.

13. *Cf. Planning Pamphlet* 23, "Public Thinking on Post-war Problems," issued by National Planning Association, October, 1943. This gives the results of public-opinion polls on a goodly number of economic

questions, but the attitude toward economic innovations, monetary or other, is not inquired into.

14. It is somewhat ironical that at the end of the same preface in which Harrod dismissed the commodity-unit idea on the grounds of the public's hesitation, he appeals strongly to the economists of Great Britain for a more receptive attitude toward new ideas.

15. *Op. cit.*, pp. 320–321.

16. Because of the objection stated, Jevons decides in favor of the "Tabular Standard," under which the amount of money payable by contract would be adjusted to reflect changes in the price of at least 100 staple articles.

It should be pointed out that in his discussion of currency convertible into a group of products, Jevons does not deal with the question of where the commodities are coming from with which to redeem the notes. The same omission is to be found in the plan of G. M. Lewis, put forward in 1925, which provides for currency convertible into a composite of wheat, cotton, iron, and silver. ("A Plan for Stabilizing Prices," *The Economic Journal*, March, 1925.)

Prof. J. P. Wernette, of Harvard University, deals in somewhat different fashion with the same underlying idea in a more recent work, *The Control of Business Cycles*, New York, 1940. Here he discusses, semiseriously, a suggested "potato standard," under which the government buys potatoes at a mint price and thus guarantees a fair market to a large number of producers in every state in the union. He then hints at the commodity-unit idea by adding, "There is, indeed, much to be said for a triple standard, consisting of hay, corn, and potatoes." Like G. M. Lewis, Wernette fails to work out the storage side of the proposal—in fact, he is quite prepared to see the potatoes destroyed—and therefore suggests later that it might be better if the government issued money in exchange for "roads, schools, battleships, and the like." As Jevons did before him, Wernette dismisses his own idea rather wistfully with the remark, "The potato standard is technically sound but psychologically impossible." (*The Control of Business Cycles*, pp. 111–114.)

Chapter VII

1. *Money and the Mechanism of Exchange*, p. 320.

2. The following tabulation shows the commodities included in various price indexes covering primary products:

Dow Jones (futures)............ Wheat, cotton, sugar, hides, corn, rubber, silk, coffee, cocoa, oats, rye. (11.)

Moody's (spot)................ Wheat, cotton, hogs, steel scrap, sugar, wool, copper, hides, corn, rubber, silk, coffee, lead, silver, cocoa. (15.)

Associated Press...............	Cement, hides, rubber, bituminous coal, petrol, steel scrap, turpentine, linseed oil, steel billets, lumber, burlap, eggs, sugar, cocoa, coffee, flour, lard, butter, hogs, cattle, lambs, corn, wheat, oats, rye, cotton, wool, rayon, cotton cloth, silk, antimony, tin, zinc, lead, copper. (35.)
Bureau of Labor Statistics (basic commodities).	Wheat, flaxseed, barley, corn, butter, tallow, hogs, steers, lard, sugar, coffee, cocoa, shellac, rubber, hides, rosin, cottonseed oil, print cloth, silk, wool tops, burlap, steel scrap, tin, copper, lead, zinc, cotton. (27.)

This should give a fair idea of the range in the number of basic commodities thought needed to represent the entire field adequately.

3. There is reason to think that lumber could be included in the composite without too great technical difficulty. *Cf.* the proposal made by Prof. C. A. Kulp that lumber be dealt in on a commodity exchange, in "Organized Commodity Markets," *Annals of the American Academy of Political and Social Science*, May, 1931, pp. 183–186.

4. See Colin Clark, *The Conditions of Economic Progress*, London, 1940, p. 56. He estimates total average income of 30 countries at 254 billion dollars, including 40 billion dollars for China and the USSR. These values include both goods and services.

5. This point is made by *The Financial News*, London, Feb. 28, 1944, p. 21 as follows: " . . . if the purchasing power of primary producing countries is maintained, the price level of manufactures will look after itself under competitive conditions."

For the converse situation, *viz.*, the distortions caused by inflexible or "administered" prices of finished goods and collapsing raw-materials prices, see G. C. Means, "Notes on Inflexible Prices," *American Economic Review, Supplement*, March, 1936, pp. 29*ff.*; also his "Report" on this subject, transmitted to the Senate by the Secretary of Agriculture, pursuant to Senate Resolution 17, Jan. 15, 1935.

6. *Cf.* the details given regarding tin-cartel quotas in *Raw Commodity Price Control*, National Industrial Conference Board Studies, No. 238, New York, 1937, pp. 136–138. Exceedingly favorable terms had to be accorded to some countries of minor importance statistically in order to bring them into the restriction scheme.

7. The plan of Prof. G. M. Lewis, referred to Note 16 to Chap. VI, considered that stabilizing a composite of four commodities only—wheat, cotton, iron, and silver—would give a satisfactory over-all stability to the dollar. Harold Fleming, in various articles in *The Christian Science Monitor* as well as in an unpublished book, has suggested that stabilization of pig iron alone would be sufficient for the purpose.

8. *Op. cit.*, p. 101.

Chapter VIII

1. *Joint Statement of Experts on the Establishment of an International Monetary Fund*, published by U.S. Treasury, Apr. 21, 1944.

2. A proposal for an *International Stabilization Fund*, etc., revised July 10, 1943, published by the U.S. Treasury.

3. British proposals for an *International Clearing Union*, Apr. 8, 1943, British Information Services, New York City (Section 39).

4. *Ibid.*, Sec. 5.

5. A selected bibliography of comment on the currency plans, issued by the International Finance Section at Princeton University, in January, 1944, lists some 70 studies and briefer articles. *Cf.* the statement of Prof. John H. Williams: "It can be said that from the time of publication of the revised White plan in August [1943] the American press and American banking and foreign trade opinion have been almost uniformly unsympathetic to both plans." (*Foreign Affairs*, January, 1944, p. 233.)

We refer also to "Tentative Draft Proposals of Canadian Experts for an International Exchange Union," Ottawa, June 9, 1943. A number of the suggestions contained in this document appear to have been followed in the Experts' Plan of Apr. 21, 1944.

Chapter IX

1. Quoted by *The Economist*, London, Dec. 11, 1943, p. 785.

2. See, *inter alia*, his address before the Chamber of Commerce of the State of New York, Feb. 3, 1944, published by the Economists National Committee on Monetary Policy, under the title, "International Currency —Gold versus Bancor or Unitas."

3. Jacob Viner, "Two Plans for International Monetary Stabilization," *Yale Review*, Autumn, 1943.

4. Hans Neisser, "An International Reserve Bank," *Social Research*, New York, September, 1943.

5. F. A. Lutz, *The Keynes-White Proposals*, Princeton University, July, 1943, p. 21.

6. Lord Keynes in *Parliamentary Debates on an International Clearing Union*, British Information Services, New York, July, 1943, p. 80.

7. *The Economist*, London, Aug. 28, 1943, pp. 261–262.

8. *Cf.* C. P. Kindelberger, "International Monetary Stabilization," in *Postwar Economic Problems*, New York, 1943, Chap. XXII. He states that "the chronic world shortage of dollars" is likely to be accentuated as a result of changes effected by the war. *Cf.*, also, *Foreign Trade after the War*, Economic Series No. 28, U.S. Department of Commerce, October, 1943.

9. *Parliamentary Debates, op. cit.*, p. 77.

10. *Cf. Golden Avalanche*, by Frank D. Graham and Charles R. Whittlesey, New York, 1939.

11. *Cf. Federal Reserve Bulletin*, April, 1944, p. 400.

12. *Cf.* article by the present author, "A Program for Gold," in *Dynamic America*, April, 1940, pp. 23*ff*.

13. Somewhat paradoxically, the opposite point has been made by Prof. E. F. Schumacher. He says that gold imports by the United States "have fulfilled exactly the same function as public works; they have served as a useful stopgap in an economy that failed to function properly." He concludes, "If the world at large, and particularly the United States, returns after the war to the unemployment and the stagnant economic system of the prewar world, the future of gold is fairly well assured. All powerful economic interests will then stand behind the gold-buying policy." "The Reconstruction Problem of Gold," *Agenda*, The London School of Economics, February, 1943, pp. 67–80.

14. See "A Commodity Reserve Currency," *The Economic Journal*, June-September, 1943, pp. 176–184.

15. Viner, *op. cit.*, p. 30.

16. F. H. Brownell, chairman, American Smelting & Refining Company, in pamphlet entitled "*International Bimetallism*," New York, 1944.

17. This attitude was again expressed in the House of Commons debates following publication of the Experts' Plan. A dispatch to *The Wall Street Journal*, discussing these debates, refers to "the anxiety lest Britain's internal economy be forced into a deflationary spiral by a rigid link with gold." (*The Wall Street Journal*, May 15, 1944, p. 1.)

The Chancellor of the Exchequer, commenting on the new proposals, averred that the attitude of the present government would be one of "most vehement opposition" to a return to a gold standard for England. (*Ibid.*, May 11, 1944, p. 1.)

18. See Appendix I, p. 142, for a brief discussion and certain data on the relative prices of farm and nonfarm raw materials.

19. This point was raised by Lord Keynes in his "Comment" on F. A. Hayek's article in *The Economic Journal* of June-September, 1943. The "Comment" is reprinted in Appendix IVC of this book, together with a reply thereto by this author (pp. 173*ff*.).

20. For a discussion of Sweden's policies between 1931 and 1939 see R. A. Lester, *Monetary Experiments*, Princeton, 1939, Chap. X. For comment on Sweden's moves to counteract inflationary pressures from the present war, see "Swedish Credit Policy," *The Economist*, London, Feb. 19, 1944, pp. 250*ff*.

21. "U.S. Treasury Proposal," *op. cit.*, V-1-c.

22. "British Proposals," *op. cit.*, 6-(8)-6.

23. *Cf.* the various Latin-American governmental debts secured by collateral *e.g.*, State of São Paolo Coffee Realization Loan, issued in 1930 and due in 1941, originally secured by 16,500,000 bags of coffee; also Department of Antioquia, Colombia, 7s, due 1945, secured by pledge

of revenues derived from the tobacco tax and by a first lien on the properties and earnings of the Antioquia Railway. When defaults occurred in these and similar loans the creditors were in general powerless, for political reasons, to enforce payment by recourse to the collateral.

Chapter X

1. *Cf.* the Scrugham Bill to provide emergency stockpiles of strategic metals, "The Mineral Stockpiles Act," S 1582, introduced Dec. 7, 1943; also the speeches and writings of W. L. Batt, vice-chairman of the War Production Board—*e.g.*, "National Emergency Stockpiles," in *Foreign Commerce Weekly,* Feb. 26, 1944, pp. 3–5, 35.

2. Address in Washington, October, 1942. But *cf.* K. E. Knorr, "Access to Raw Materials in the Post-war World," *Harvard Business Review,* Spring, 1943. In critical vein he calls "equal access" a phrase coined to meet an "equally meaningless slogan coined by the Axis powers—the distinction between the 'Have' and the 'Have-not' nations" (p. 787).

3. *Cf.* articles by Hansen and Condliffe, referred to in Note 1 to Chap. VI.

4. *Wall Street Journal,* Jan. 16, 1944, p. 1.

5. A portion of this last idea is included in earlier proposals for an "international raw-materials commission to control the distribution of raw materials needed for modern industry in such a way that no nation can accumulate stocks for use in war . . . ." (Vera M. Dean, *Foreign Policy Reports,* No. 22, Feb. 1, 1943.) This approach is treated at some length in the concluding chapter of *World Minerals and World Peace,* The Brookings Institution, 1943.

6. The commission's text on this suggestion is as follows: "A commodity corporation could coordinate purchases, accumulate materials and direct their use both for war purposes and for reconstruction purposes following the war. Such an agency could absorb world surpluses and release them when occasion favored and need required." (*Third Report,* February, 1943.)

7. See *Preliminary Draft Outline of a Proposal for a United Nations Bank for Reconstruction and Development,* U.S. Treasury, November, 1943.

8. For references thereto in the White and Keynes plans, see Notes 2 and 3 to Chap. VIII. Prof. J. H. Williams has called attention to the importance of viewing the currency plans in relation to the broader program, which includes "measures for stabilizing the prices of primary products in international trade." (*Foreign Affairs,* January, 1944, p. 247.)

9. *Cf.* "Stabilized Reflation," *The Economic Forum,* Spring, 1933; *Storage and Stability—A Modern Ever-normal Granary,* New York, 1937, both by this author.

10. See Alvin Johnson's Preface to *Storage and Stability.*

11. See Frank D. Graham, *Social Goals and Economic Institutions*, Princeton University, 1942; *Fundamentals of International Monetary Policy*, reprinted by The Monetary Standards Inquiry, New York, October, 1943; and numerous articles in the *American Economic Journal* and elsewhere.

Frank Graham is undoubtedly the second father of commodity-reserve currency. I am happy that the accidental similarity of our names has identified both of us indistinguishably with the proposal. *Ambos una manet laus*, I trust.

12. W. I. King, *The Causes of Economic Fluctuations*, New York, 1938, p. 304.

13. R. A. Lester, *Monetary Experiments*, Princeton University, 1939, pp. 299–305.

14. E. E. Agger, "Money and Banking Today," New York, 1941.

15. H. L. Reed, *Money, Currency, and Banking*, Chap. XXXIX.

16. "A Commodity Reserve Currency," *The Economic Journal*, June–September, 1943.

17. Replies to the "Critique" by Frank D. Graham and myself were published in *The Journal of Political Economy*, February, 1943. Considerations of space preclude reprinting here of F. D. Graham's article. My remarks on Lord Keynes' comment, printed in the Appendix IV, have not been published elsewhere.

18. The elaborate study of J. E. Reeves, *Monetary Reform Movements*, pp. 358–362, 388, Washington, 1943, contains a fairly comprehensive discussion of commodity-reserve currency. The criticisms of the plan, on the one hand, relate to (1) problems of administration, (2) its relative effectiveness as an antidepression measure, (3) its diversion of production into a limited part of the economy, (4) the costs of storage (admittedly of minor importance), and (5) the possible need for a "redistribution of income" to offset expansion of the commodity reserves.

On the other hand, Reeves grants that the plan "has distinct merit" as an extension of the principle of symmetallism by the use of "numerous other commodities more important than silver or gold." In his conclusion Reeves expresses doubts as to the future of both precious metals as world currency. He adds, "Of the miscellaneous monetary proposals the strongest future possibilities appear to lie in some of the antihoarding schemes, as well as in Benjamin Graham's composite currency plan. Wartime experiences with shortages of basic metals, moreover, may bring additional appeal for combining commodity reserves with the monetary standard" (p. 388).

19. Address at the twenty-ninth National Foreign Trade Convention, Boston, Oct. 7–9, 1942.

20. *The New York Sun*, June 1, 1943.

21. *The New International Wheat Agreements*, Food Research Institute, Stanford University, 1943, Sec. IV.

22. *Ibid*, p. 54.

23. Suggestions for national stockpiles, already referred to, have been made by Senator J. C. Scrugham, W. L. Batt, R. J. Scanlan, L. S. Grondona. Other proposals along the same lines include the following:

Prof. Jan Goudriaan, of the Commercial University of Rotterdam, published a pamphlet in 1932, entitled "How to Stop Deflation" (printed in London by The Search Publishing Company), in which he sets forth a proposal for central-bank operations in commodity reserves on a composite basis. His suggestion is in all essential respects identical with the one advanced in this book, which was first published in the United States in 1933.

Prof. H. F. Otte, of Columbia University, has suggested that postwar repayment of lend-lease take the form of raw materials to be stockpiled for future emergencies.

Max Stern, a New York businessman, proposed that we establish at least one year's stockpile of all war-needed metals. He suggests, further, that metal ingots other than gold be added to the backing of our currency —on the ground that these metals would contribute more than gold to the safety of our country. (See article *The New York Times*, Nov. 14, 1943.)

Several years ago Prof. R. B. Harvey, of the University of Minnesota, proposed "a super-normal granary," consisting of 12 billion dollars of many foods, to be stored almost indefinitely by the use of improved techniques. (See article by Watson Davis in *New York World-Telegram*, Dec. 30, 1937; also "Super-normal Granary," *Science News Letter*, Jan. 21, 1939, pp. 42–43.)

J. Maynard Keynes proposed in 1938 that Great Britain establish large stockpiles to assure her position in the event of war and also to promote economic stability. (See his address, "The Policy of Government Storage of Foodstuffs and Raw Materials," in The *Economic Journal*, September, 1938.)

Stockpiles to be held by an *international* agency have been favored by Keynes, Hansen, J. S. Davis, the Committee to Study the Organization of Peace, the Federation of Master Cotton Spinners Associations in England, and many others.

24. See H. G. Moulton, *Income and Economic Progress*, The Brookings Institution, Washington, 1935.

25. This viewpoint is illustrated by the following remark of Dr. E. A. Goldenweiser: "I am inclined to think that even business stability—which is a vague term describing the goal toward which, in a general way, everyone should try to work—is not necessarily desirable. Stability has an

implication of stagnation. A growing economy is not a stable economy." ("How Can Credit be Controlled?" *Proceedings of the Academy of Political Science*, May, 1936, p. 8.)

26. *Cf.* references to this objective in Secretary Morgenthau's Foreword to the Revised White Plan, July 10, 1943, and in the body of the Keynes Plan (quoted Chap. VIII, p. 86).

27. Published by The Foreign Policy Association, New York, 1934.

28. This is the financing method suggested in the Goudriaan and Scanlan proposals, discussed in Note 6, Chap. VI and Note 23, Chap. X. Also *cf.* Keynes's suggestion that his proposed Clearing Union "might finance stocks of commodities" held by a Commodity Control. (Sec. 39–3 of Proposals for an International Clearing Union, *op. cit.*)

29. Address of the Hon. W. Chatfield-Taylor, before the World Trade Luncheon, New York, May 18, 1942, p. 8.

30. *Cf.* "A Commodity Reserve Currency," *op. cit.*, p. 184.

31. Reprinted by The Economists National Committee on Monetary Policy, New York, 1943.

32. Prof. W. E. Spahr also uses this quotation from the Macmillan Committee Report in his pamphlet, *Alternatives in Postwar Monetary Standards*, published by The Monetary Standards Inquiry, New York, January, 1944. His discussion of the various alternatives to the orthodox gold standard includes a "critique" of commodity-reserve currency, consisting of no more than the following single paragraph:

"Any attempt to create an international paper money based upon commodities other than metallic currencies (*a commodity money standard*) would lead to failure because such a plan ignores a basic *sine qua non* of a good paper money—redeemability in a metallic money of universal acceptability" (p. 18).

In other words, commodity-reserve money is no good because it is not gold money. Q.E.D.

33. This is the author's view, shared by a large number of economists who believe that in recent years the value of gold has depended upon its dollar price rather than vice versa. Naturally, the gold-standard adherents would dispute this statement.

34. *Op. cit.*, Chap. XI, point 14.

35. *Monetary Reform in Theory and Practice*, London, 1936, p. 209.

36. *The Times*, London, Feb. 15, 1943, p. 3.

37. *Foreign Commerce Weekly*, Sept. 25, 1943, p. 17.

38. *The Financial News*, London, Feb. 1, 1944, p. 2.

39. *The Times*, London, July 8, 1942, p. 5.

40. *The Financial News*, London, Dec. 14, 1943, p. 1.

41. *Cf.* W. I. King, *The Causes of Economic Fluctuations*, *op. cit.*

42. These include Prof. W. I. King, Prof. Valdemar Carlson, Rep. Jerry Voorhis, etc.

43. *Agenda for a Post-war World*, New York, 1942, p. 202.

44. *Cf.* the thoughtful pamphlet of Lever Bros. on "The Problem of Unemployment," London, 1943. This suggests that both industry and government follow measures designed to assure regularity in the rate of extension of capital equipment (pp. 12–16).

This principle has been adopted in the British Government's White Paper on Employment Policy, published May 26, 1944.

45. The Guaranty Trust Company of New York conducted a poll of businessmen in early 1944 to determine their views on a number of matters of governmental policy. Its summary of the results of the poll includes the following statement: "Many businessmen see a continuing threat in the idea that deficit spending by the government can stimulate business enterprise." (*The New York Times*, May 20, 1944, p. 28.)

46. *Cf.* the following statement in the "Critique," by Messrs. Beale, Kennedy, and Winn, Appendix IV:

"Cognizance may be taken also of other devices such as taxation and fiscal policy, which may be used to regulate price fluctuations. It seems probable, in fact, that these measures may be made to provide a quicker and more efficient method of dealing with this problem than that which commodity reserve currency offers." (Their footnote 14.)

47. *Op. cit.*, p. 59.

48. In the Foreword to *Storage and Stability*, Dr. Alvin Johnson said, "The invention is of such startling simplicity that everyone who examines it must feel that he once had the idea himself" (p. xvi).

49. See the discussion on this point by Frank Graham, in "Commodity Reserve Currency: A Criticism of the Critique," *Journal of Political Economy*, February, 1943, pp. 71–72. He concludes, "In fact, the only possible safeguard of liberty is the diffusion of liberty among self-interested groups, with a lively consciousness on the part of all that the public treasury, or the public income, cannot be plundered by any group except at the expense of others. This education in the obvious would be of immense aid in improving our political life."

50. Current legislation calls for the distribution of 500 million dollars a year for three years to the various states for interstate highways. The formula proposed is a little more complicated than formerly. A weight of 50 per cent is to be given to population, 25 per cent to area, and 25 per cent to road mileage. In addition, 70 per cent is to go to rural areas and 30 per cent to cities. (See article in *Business Week*, June 10, 1944, p. 34.)

51. Quoted from *Report of Section III, United Nations Conference on Food and Agriculture*.

APPENDIX I

Data Re World Production and Exports of Raw Materials

SUMMARY OF THE WORLD'S RAW-MATERIAL PRODUCTION, 1937 (EXCLUDING RUSSIA AND CHINA)

Approximate Dollar Values, Based on United States Prices

Commodity	World production		United States production, millions of dollars	United States net imports, millions of dollars
	Quantity, thous. of metric tons	Value, millions of dollars		
1. Commodities in proposed unit:				
Wheat.............	103,600	$ 4,330	$ 981	
Corn..............	117,400	3,080	1,776	
Cotton............	8,300	1,950	1,137	
Wool (grease).......	1,710	1,080	130	$ 96
Rubber............	1,160	470	.....	249
Coffee.............	2,480	330	.....	151
Tea...............	460	230	.....	21
Sugar.............	27,430	1,430	148	166
Tobacco...........	2,440	1,230	500	
Total agricultural..	264,980	$14,130	$4,672	$ 683
Petroleum.........	279,900	$ 2,440	$1,587	
Coal..............	1,307,400	5,250	2,000	
Wood pulp........	24,260	1,050	273	$ 98
Pig iron...........	104,000	2,070	853	
Copper............	2,340	640	217	
Tin...............	200	230	.....	104
Total industrial....	2,718,100	$11,680	$4,930	$ 202
Total in unit......	2,983,080	$25,810	$9,602	$ 885
2. First rank commodities—probably adaptable to composite:				
Lumber............	....	$ 3,000 (est.)	$ 637	
Oats..............	47,410	1,260	350	
Rice..............	93,940	4,790	45	
Total.............	....	$ 9,050	$1,032	

SUMMARY OF THE WORLD'S RAW-MATERIAL PRODUCTION, 1937 (EXCLUDING RUSSIA AND CHINA).—(*Continued*)

Commodity	World production		United States production, millions of dollars	United States net imports, millions of dollars
	Quantity, thous. of metric tons	Value, millions of dollars		
3. First rank commodities—probably not adaptable to composite:				
Dairy products (including eggs and poultry).........	....	$10,000 (est.)	$2,500	
Meat products......	....	10,000 (est.)	2,500	
Total.............	....	$20,000	$5,000	
4. Second rank commodities:				
Barley.............	32,780	$ 900	$ 175	
Rye...............	22,600	840	37	
Rayon.............	5,450	600	252	
Cottonseed (products).............	16,900	470	229	
Cement...........	79,900	400	171	$ 1
Olive oil...........	1,120	360	..:...	9
Flax..............	810	330	.....	3
Margarine.........	1,290	300	60	
Aluminum.........	490	250	56	
Soybeans..........	6,640	250	40	
Zinc..............	1,620	210	72	
Silk..............	54	170	.....	107
Lead..............	1,690	160	55	
Jute and burlaps....	1,580	150	.....	52
Flaxseed...........	2,550	140	15	35
Copra.............	1,680	140	.....	3
Salt..............	37,000	100 (est.)	27	
Total.............	....	$ 5,770	$1,189	$ 210
5. Third rank commodities:				
Cocoa.............	700	$ 90	.....	$ 53
Hemp.............	265	80	.....	
Manganese.........	2,970	90	$ 5	13
Nickel.............	114	90	.....	24
Phosphates.........	10,572	60	13	
Sulphur...........	3,400	70	44	

SUMMARY OF THE WORLD'S RAW-MATERIAL PRODUCTION, 1937 (EXCLUDING RUSSIA
AND CHINA).—(*Continued*)

Commodity	World production		United States production, millions of dollars	United States net imports, millions of dollars
	Quantity, metric tons	Value, millions of dollars		
5. Third rank commodities: (*Continued*)				
Potash............	3,100	$ 50	$ 9	$ 14
Palm oil...........	503	40	.....	16
Manila hemp.......	200	30	.....	8
Molybdenum.......	15	23	16	
Chrome............	590	20	.....	7
Antimony..........	42*	10	.....	2
Magnesium.........	20	12	.....	
Mercury...........	5	10	2	1
Platinum...........	400†	15	.....	
Tungsten...........	22*	26	4	3
Total............	....	$ 716	$ 93	$ 141
Grand total of non-monetary raw materials..............		About $62,000	About $17,000	About $1,300
6. Monetary metals:				
Gold..............	30‡	$ 1,042	$ 168	$1,586
Silver.............	275‡	124	56	80
Total............	....	$ 1,166	$ 224	$1,666

* Includes China.
† Thousand ounces.
‡ Million ounces.

Note: This summary includes all the commodities listed in the League of Nations *Statistical Year Book* for 1938 with the exception of a few with value less than 10 million dollars. Some additional data are taken from *World Minerals and World Peace*, Washington, 1943.

The values given are approximations based largely on United States import or export prices. They are intended to present a fairly accurate picture of the structure of the world's raw materials economy.

APPENDIX II

Relative Price Movements within and without the Proposed Commodity Unit

Critical students of the commodity-reserve proposal have raised various questions regarding its objective of price stability. Their doubts have been expressed on two main points: first, whether a stable value of the units will stabilize sufficiently the prices of its components; second, whether it will stabilize sufficiently all other elements of the price structure.

On the first point, it is a prime thesis of this plan that individual prices should be left free to fluctuate both temporarily and secularly. We do believe that over-all price stability will diminish considerably the range of fluctuations in individual components, in addition to which the replacement of spots by futures at a discount will prevent a great deal of speculative manipulation. Day-to-day changes in commodity prices are normal and not unwholesome; while long-term changes in relative prices are both normal and basically inevitable. What is disruptive and completely harmful is the alternation of wide upswings and severe collapses of the raw-materials price level as a whole.

Passing from individual commodities to groups of products, some fear has been expressed lest the industrial components in the unit may advance over the years while the agricultural portion may decline in value. This is theoretically possible, just as the reverse is possible, and it may be accepted on the ground that it would be a normal reflection of supply and demand developments within the unit. It is more realistic to point out that such divergent price movements of the two subgroups have not actually occurred to any substantial degree in the past, which might indicate that they are scarcely a probability for the future.

Mr. Louis H. Bean has been kind enough to supply this author with the results of elaborate studies made in the price movements of individual and group components of the *Sauerbeck-Statist Index of Basic Commodity Prices* (London). These may be taken as a reasonably good reflection of world prices. We may, for practical purposes, assume that the grouping "All Foods"—comprising 19 articles—will cover the agricultural field. while the grouping "All Materials"—comprising the remaining 26 articles—will cover the industrial field. Actually, the inclusion of eight textiles in "All Materials" introduces an agricultural element into the latter.

Two interesting conclusions emerge from Mr. Bean's figures. The first is that during the last 60 years there has been only a moderate secular change in the relative position of the two main subgroups. Taking 1867–1877 values as a base, we find that during the period 1921–1940 the average price for the food group was some 6 per cent lower and that of the materials group some 4 per cent higher than two generations before. If this relative movement were duplicated over the next 60 years, the agricultural producers could scarcely complain of serious hardship.

The second conclusion is that both subgroups showed very much the same relative price changes from year to year during the wide swings of 1921–1940. In these years the index itself declined from 155 to 79 and recovered to 128. Yet the food index never fluctuated more than 9 percentage points from its average or normal position in relation to the total index, and the materials index stayed correspondingly close to its normal position in nearly every year.

It would seem to be a reasonable conclusion, since even under conditions of great general disturbance the two groups fluctuated in close harmony, that they are not likely to move in widely different directions when the over-all price index remains stable. This inference is strengthened by the observation that during the relatively stable years 1922–1929 (while the general index varied between 115 and 139) the "All Foods" group did not deviate more than 5 per cent from its normal or 20-year average position.

The second point bears upon the relation of commodity-unit prices to other prices. It can easily be shown that fluctuations in the value of our 15-commodity unit have paralleled closely those in much more comprehensive indexes, especially if rubber is excluded from the unit value because of its particularly high 1913–1914 price. This would be true even if the unit were constructed along somewhat different lines, e.g., if it were based upon United States production and foreign trade instead of upon world figures. The following table will support these statements:

VARIATIONS IN INDEXES OF WHOLESALE PRICES IN SELECTED YEARS (1926 = 100)

Year	Bureau of Labor Statistics Index			14-Commodity unit (excluding rubber)	
	All commodities	Raw materials	Farm products	World basis	United States basis
1913–1914	69	68	71	65	64
1920	154	152	151	193	195
1922	97	96	94	98	101
1926	100	100	100	100	100
1932	65	55	48	53	52
1937	86	85	86	80	79
1938	79	72	69	73	72

Aside from the special weakness of farm products in 1932, the only large variation in these figures is found in the year 1920 when the 14 unit commodities advanced to a level about 30 per cent higher than the more comprehensive indexes. (Note: There are now about 890 items in the Bureau of Labor Statistics all-commodity index and 110 in its raw-materials index.)

With respect to the interrelationship of basic-commodity prices and other prices, the following is an illuminative quotation from the description of the *General Motors-Cornell World Price Index*, p. 3:

"It is significant that whenever wide price movements occur, regardless of the cause, the prices of certain universal basic commodities fluctuate far more rapidly, and to a far greater extent, than do those of most other goods. It is likewise significant that approximately 80 per cent of the persons gainfully employed in the world are engaged directly in the production, processing, and distribution of 40 to 50 of these universal basic commodities and their derivative products."

APPENDIX III

The Storage Aspect of Commodity-reserve Currency

There are four basic questions regarding storage of commodity units, *viz.*,
1. Can the units be stored indefinitely?
2. What is the annual storage cost per dollar unit?
3. What will be the average over-all cost of storage?
4. How will this cost be defrayed?

The following discussion will attempt to throw some light on these questions. Lack of available data and of completed research prevents a thoroughly comprehensive treatment of the subject at this time.

I. STORABILITY OF THE UNITS

There are no physical problems of storage involved in this proposal other than those that may be stated in terms of moderate expense. All the component commodities have actually been held in large reserve stocks on a continuing basis; in fact, they have been selected with that criterion in mind. The care needed to be given to the stored products will naturally vary with the item. Some—like the metals—need virtually no attention; others require periodical turning or shifting to keep them in good condition. The basic principle for maintaining merchantable stocks of semiperishables is that of rotation, which means shipping the product out into consumption before deterioration sets in and replacing it by the current crop. The only expense involved here is that of warehouse handling. Since, in the typical case, there is a corresponding warehouse expense with respect to the new crop commodity, rotation should not involve appreciable financial cost in an integrated storage system.

A good deal of information on the physical aspects of large-scale storage is contained in an article, "Super-normal Granary," by Dr. Frank Thone, in *Science News Letter*, Jan. 21, 1939. This article discusses Prof. R. B. Harvey's proposal for a 12 billion dollar commodity reserve and indicates that by proper techniques it would be possible to store a wide variety of products at comparatively small expense. It is suggested, for example, that both coal and lumber may be stored under water with a minimum of deterioration.

II. COST OF STORAGE PER DOLLAR OF COMMODITY UNITS

In 1937 the present author made a preliminary study of the cost of storing a 23-commodity unit, and concluded that it would come to about 3 per cent of value per annum. (See table on p. 108 of *Storage and Stability*.) Lord Keynes's address on "The Policy of Government Storage of Food-stuffs and Raw Materials" (reprinted in *The Economic Journal*, September, 1938) estimated the cost at about 4 per cent, *including interest*. Further study suggests that my 1937 estimate was on the high side, and that the proposed 15-commodity unit could be stored in the producing countries at an annual cost of not more than 2 per cent of the unit's value. For example, information now at hand indicates that the cost of storing coffee in Brazil by the National Coffee Department is less than 1 per cent of its value as against about 3 per cent in our 1937 table.

III. AVERAGE STORAGE EXPENSE INVOLVED IN THE COMMODITY-RESERVE PLAN

In Chap. V we calculated that the average value of the commodities in the reserve would range from 5 to 7 billion dollars. On this point it may be noted that Prof. Goudriaan estimated that the excessive world stocks of all the prominent raw materials in 1932 had a value *at* 1928 *prices* of less than 5 billion dollars. (*How to Stop Deflation*, London, 1932, Appendix III.) At an average storage expense of 2 per cent per annum the yearly cost of the proposal would come to about 100 to 150 million dollars.

If this estimate is anywhere near the truth, it would be fair to say that the expense of storage is a completely minor element in the proposal. Set against the scope of the world economy, and weighed against the advantages of stability and expansion that we claim will result from the commodity reservoir, its money cost can be virtually ignored. Stated differently, if the plan has any appreciable merits they will overshadow the storage charges; if the plan is to be rejected it must be for reasons other than such expense.

It should be remarked, besides, that most of the storage costs here involved will be incurred in any case—either by operation of normal commercial storage procedures or by buffer-stock policies carried on by governments. In the ultimate sense most of this storage will involve scarcely any true economic cost since it will utilize structures that will otherwise be vacant and labor of a type that is likely otherwise to be unemployed.

IV. METHODS OF MEETING THE MONEY COST OF STORAGE

The IMF—or other agency operating the commodity reserve—will have at least five separate sources from which storage costs can be met.

The first is the proposed arrangement for free storage by vendor nations for a limited period—say, two years. The second is the option accorded to member nations to assume physical custody of their proportion of the commodity units at their own charge. It seems probable that many nations will wish to hold their share of the fund's commodity units as well as of the fund's gold. This will give them emergency reserves of essential commodities at a cost confined to storage, *i.e.*, without interest expense—and on a basis that segregates them from commercial stocks and the commercial markets except when the price level would otherwise be advancing above the stabilized level.

The third way of meeting storage costs is by the seigniorage, or price differential between the buying and selling points. This has been set, provisionally, at 10 per cent—although a considerably smaller spread may be found preferable. How much profit will be realized by these standard operations of buying and selling can only be conjectured. If half of the reserve were "turned" in this manner once every seven years—a perhaps not unreasonable supposition—the resultant gain would defray about one-third of the total storage costs.

A further source of income will be supplied by special operations in individual commodities comprising the replacement of spots by futures at a discount. Judging by the behavior of the American markets, opportunities in this direction will be rather frequent. These operations will be desirable not only as a source of income but as a means of using the commodities in the reserve to alleviate temporary shortages in single products. To make this point clearer it should be said that the underlying soundness of the commodity reserve will be in no wise impaired by these forward operations. The spot commodity will be replaced temporarily by good futures contracts together with deposit of the funds necessary to pay for the goods on delivery. Incidentally, each of these switches will constitute a rotation and thus will help keep the commodities in merchantable condition.

To the extent that storage costs are not defrayed by the four methods above listed they will form part of the operating expenses of the proposed IMF and they will be met in the same manner as its other expenses—presumably by assessment on an equitable basis. We submit the conclusion that these assessed expenditures will constitute only a minor proportion of a total storage burden which is itself of secondary importance.

APPENDIX IV-A

Commodity Reserve Currency: a Critique

W. T. M. BEALE, JR., M. T. KENNEDY, AND W. J. WINN

Reprinted from *The Journal of Political Economy*, August, 1942, pp. 579–594, by permission of the authors, the University of Chicago Press, and the *Journal of Political Economy*.

During the last two decades a number of proposals have been made relating variously to the storage of surplus commodities, the use of basic commodities as backing for money, and the stabilization of the price level.[1] The more pertinent of the ideas contained in these proposals have recently been synthesized in a plan for a commodity reserve currency, whereby monetary status would be given a composite group of primary commodities.[2] Increasing efforts have been made to bring this plan to the attention of the public, and it has received favorable attention from a number of professional economists.[3] It is proposed in the following pages

[1] Attempts to deal with the problems arising after the first World War (1914–1918 were productive of several proposals; see the discussion of the Edison plan for a com modity dollar by Garet Garrett, *New York Times*, July 16, 1922; testimony of Sir Charles Fielding (Dec. 31, 1924) and E. F. Wise (Jan. 8, 1925) before the Royal Commission on Food Prices; Gilbert N. Lewis, "A Plan for Stabilizing Prices," *Economic Journal*, March, 1925; D. H. Robertson, *Banking Policy and the Price Level*, London, 1926, pp. 96–99.

[2] The most detailed analysis of the plan is presented by Benjamin Graham in his book, *Storage and Stability*, New York, 1937. The plan was first presented in Mr. Graham's article, "Stabilized Reflation," *Economic Forum*, Vol. I, No. 2, Spring, 1933. The most recent analysis by Mr. Graham is "Storage and Stability—a Plan for Monetizing the Commodity Surplus," in *A Forum on Finance*, New York, 1940.

[3] The following articles deal with the Graham proposal or phases of a similar idea: Frank D. Graham, "The Primary Functions of Money and Their Consummation in Monetary Policy," *American Economic Review Supplement*, March, 1940, and "Transition to a Commodity Reserve Currency," *American Economic Review*, September, 1941; Hans R. L. Cohrssen, a review of *Storage and Stability* in *Dynamic America*, March, 1938; Richard A. Lester, *Monetary Experiments*, Princeton, 1939, pp. 299–305; Paul Einzig, *Monetary Reform: Theory and Practice*, London, 1936, pp. 201–9; Elmer C. Bratt, *Business Cycles and Forecasting*, Chicago, 1940; John Maynard Keynes, "The Policy of Government Storage of Foodstuffs and Raw Materials," *Economic Journal*, September, 1938; J. M. Clark, "The Proposal for a Com-

to review the theoretical bases of the plan and to examine the effects which might be expected to follow the establishment of such a currency.

THE PLAN

The basic elements of the plan for a commodity reserve currency may be summarized briefly. First, a composite unit would be formed consisting of a carefully weighted group of basic raw materials[4]—such units to be acquired and stored by the state "when there is a surplus of these commodities in the aggregate."[5] Secondly, this composite unit would be accorded monetary status by providing for two-way convertibility: paper currency would be issued in exchange for composite units, and composite units would be exchanged for paper currency. Thirdly, this free convertibility would provide the basis for automatic regulation of the supply of basic money. Expansion of the supply of such money would be achieved by the surrender to a central monetary authority, corresponding to the mint, of multiples of the composite unit, and contraction of the supply would be brought about by the presentation of notes in exchange for commodities in amounts determined by the composite unit.[6] Finally, the commodities acquired and stored by the state would provide a reservoir to be drawn upon in emergency, such as war or drought.

There is a close analogy between the mechanism of this plan and that of the gold standard in that it would accord to a composite group of basic commodities exactly the same monetary status as was given to gold under the classic gold standard. Essentially, the two standards differ only in that specified quantities of basic raw materials in the composite unit would replace a specified number of grains of gold in the dollar.

---

posite Commodity Currency," *Economics Essays in Honour of Gustav Cassel*, London, 1933, pp. 75–87; George de Bothezat, *The Depression: Its Real Causes and the Remedy*, New York, 1933.

[4] Benjamin Graham includes the following twenty-three commodities: corn, wheat, sugar, oats, coffee, barley, rye, cocoa, cottonseed oil, cotton, wool, silk, copper, lead, tin, zinc, petroleum, hides, rubber, cottonseed meal, flaxseed, tobacco, tallow (*Storage and Stability*, pp. 53–54). Frank D. Graham states that "I would be inclined greatly to enlarge the list of commodities in the composite unit used as a monetary standard as compared with what Mr. Benjamin Graham, in the interest of administrative convenience, has suggested" (*American Economic Review Supplement*, March, 1940, p. 13).

[5] Benjamin Graham, *Storage and Stability*, p. 49.

[6] Currency would be issued whenever the aggregate market value of the component items included in the unit was such as to permit the purchase of the various units at a cost slightly under their standard, or "coinage," value, and commodity units would be redeemed whenever the aggregate market value of the component items was slightly above the standard value.

PURPORTED ADVANTAGES OF THE PLAN

Among the various advantages which, it is maintained, might be expected to result from the adoption of the plan are several which merit especial attention. First, it is claimed that the plan would operate automatically in the same sense and in substantially the same way as the free gold standard. Secondly, it is contended that the monetizing of a composite commodity unit would stabilize the collective price of the commodities included in the unit in exactly the same manner as the fixed mint price stabilized the price of gold. (It should be noted, in this connection, that the prices of the individual commodities would be free to fluctuate within the limits set by stabilization of the composite unit; but it is argued that the stabilization of the collective price of the commodities included in the unit would have a powerful stabilizing effect on the general level of prices.) Thirdly, the assurance of a stable price for the composite unit in a period when other prices were declining would, presumably, tend to stimulate production of the commodities included in the unit and benefit producers of those commodities, just as under the free gold standard a fall in the price level was assumed to afford an immediate and considerable stimulus to the gold-mining industry. The stimulus afforded to a large segment of the national economy would be expected to provide a powerful impetus to general business activity. Fourthly, the building-up of a reservoir of basic agricultural materials is viewed as assuring at least a partial solution of the farm problem by providing an outlet for surplus products. This would be of particular importance during the period of transition to the plan but would, in addition, become operative during any period of depression and falling prices. This follows from the preceding point. Finally, the accumulation of raw materials as monetary reserves would involve the creation of stores which could be drawn upon in emergencies.

Before an attempt is made to pass upon the validity of these claims, certain problems pertinent to the merits of the plan itself will be examined; while primary emphasis will be directed toward its economic aspects, some recognition will necessarily be given to political considerations.

PROBLEMS RELATING TO THE DOMESTIC MONETARY ASPECTS
OF COMMODITY RESERVE CURRENCY

Transition

The introduction of a new type of money may involve the replacement of all existing forms of currency, the substitution of the new currency for some of the existing forms, or merely the addition of the new currency to existing forms. The proponents of the plan assume the first of these alternatives to be the ideal policy, but they recognize that the supplanting of all forms of money with commodity reserve currency would meet with great opposition.[7] The second alternative—namely, the substitution of the commodity currency for existing forms of money—is also rejected except in so far as Federal Reserve notes may be replaced "to the extent that such notes are no longer needed."[8] By a process of elimination, then, the addition of the new currency to existing forms is offered as the principal method of effecting the transition to a commodity reserve currency system.

The points at issue in a discussion of the problems of transition may be clarified by keeping in mind the fundamental similarities between the commodity reserve system and the traditional gold standard. In order for a commodity currency, whether gold or commodity reserve currency, to function effectively it is not necessary, according to the theory, that all money be fully backed or that the currency in circulation be limited to the basic type. It is essential, however, that the commodity currency constitute *a sufficient portion of the total to allow for any contraction and that all expansion be effected through the commodity currency*. The monetary supply would then be regulated by movements into and out of reserves. It is obvious that this method of adjustment represents an application of the principle of an uncovered issue, which was a characteristic feature of the gold standard as maintained in England. Transition on a scale such as this represents the minimum requirement that must be met under the plan as proposed.[9]

The first question to be considered in connection with transition of the scale indicated relates to the existing types of money, *viz.*, gold and silver certificates, Federal Reserve notes, United States notes, and demand deposits. Any one or all of these might be retained as the uncovered issue, but the amount outstanding must either be fixed or be held to a fixed

[7] In the *American Economic Review* for September, 1941, Frank D. Graham has undertaken to discuss the transition to a commodity reserve currency. Unfortunately, this article is also concerned with a number of other questions, including the general merits of the plan and issues relating to bank policy, and fails to shed as much light as might be hoped on the problems of transition.

[8] "The commodity-backed money is not intended to replace other currency—except Federal Reserve notes, to the extent these are no longer needed. It will be one more form of money added to the ten existing types. True, we have too many kinds already; but the addition of still another may be excused if thus we establish a sensible and helpful relationship between our currency structure and our national product" (Benjamin Graham, *Forum on Finance*, p. 177).

[9] It may be noted in passing that transition on this minimum scale would reduce, as compared with transition on a less restricted scale, the time, expense, and inconvenience of establishing the system and likewise would relieve the technical problems of storage and costs. On the other hand, it would likewise limit the contribution it would make to the accumulation of emergency stocks and to providing an outlet for surplus stocks.

reserve ratio. If the transition to commodity reserve currency is to achieve its objectives, a strong and unified control over the other elements in the total circulating medium is essential,[10] for, otherwise, changes in the monetary supply might result from changes in any one of its components. Thus the effect of changes in the supply of commodity money might be negated by changes in the supply of other types of money.

Another issue relates to the time at which transition is effected. The most opportune time for inaugurating the new currency system would appear to be the beginning of a depression. The process of acquiring and storing commodities would obviously create a demand for basic raw materials. The contribution this would make toward solving the problem of surplus production, which has been described as the "real objective" of the plan,[11] would presumably be greatest at the onset of a depression when demand would otherwise be declining. If an ensuing turn of the business cycle should reverse this process, it would become necessary to assure that any retirement of currency was confined to other forms of money. Otherwise, the completion of the cycle would return the currency structure to its original status, and the transition to commodity currency would have proved abortive.

Operation of the Plan

The benefits of monetary reform may presumably be sought by way of either a managed monetary standard or an automatically operated standard. Recent monetary history seems to indicate a trend away from automatism toward management; but it can hardly be denied that, if the same benefits can be obtained under an automatic as under a managed monetary standard, the former is to be preferred. This preference is based in part on recognition of the difficulty of securing competent management by fallible human beings: difficult decisions must be made, frequently based upon inadequate information; administration may devolve upon incompetent officials; the temptation to pander to political considerations may overcome resistance; and public confidence may be shaken. One of the principal arguments advanced in support of the plan for a commodity reserve currency, therefore, is that it would operate automatically, once the commodities to be included in the composite unit were determined and their relative weights were established. As mentioned earlier, the pattern of automatism is that, whenever the aggregate market value of the component items included in the composite unit was slightly less than their standard value, currency would be issued; and whenever the aggregate market value was slightly above their standard value, commodity units would be retired.

[10] Frank D. Graham, *American Economic Review*, September, 1941, p. 521.
[11] Benjamin Graham, *Storage and Stability*, p. 67.

Since its alleged automatism occupies so prominent a place in the argument, it is necessary to call attention to the significance of certain further features of the plan. Advocates of an automatic system can hardly fail to be disturbed by the suggestions for (a) periodic revision of the unit, (b) substitution of futures for spot commodities under certain circumstances, and (c) the absorption of reserves into commodity uses in case of emergency.[12] Each of these features obviously represents a departure from automatism. Administrative decisions would be involved in choosing the time and method of revising the unit and the time for substituting futures for commodities. Resort to these measures would constitute the surrender of automatism and the introduction of monetary management.[13] The use of the basic raw materials composing the monetary reserve for emergency relief or military requirements is likewise incompatible with automatism. Moreover, the possibility that the basic monetary reserve could be dissipated whenever the need arose would seem to remove the very protection a monetary reserve is designed to afford.

Supporters of the present proposal are entitled to advocate, as they wish, monetary automatism or monetary management, but they are scarcely justified in marrying the two in this cavalier fashion. They can scarcely expect to arouse great enthusiasm for a plan which preaches the virtues of the automatic standard, while containing elements categorically incompatible with automatism.

The Problem of Price Stabilization

It is claimed that the commodity reserve currency plan would tend to stabilize the general price level by providing a mechanism for stabilizing the price level of the basic commodities included in the monetary unit. It is recognized of course that the plan, even though it provided stability for the composite unit price, would by no means prevent fluctuations in the prices of the components of the unit. The constituent prices would be free to vary with changing economic conditions; and as the prices changed the relative-value composition of the unit would change. Suppose, for example, that a bumper wheat harvest resulted in lower wheat prices. Under the commodity reserve currency system the decline in the price of wheat would cause additional commodity units to be monetized until some or all of the prices of the other commodities in the unit had risen enough to offset the lower price of wheat. Thus commodity currency would probably prevent the price of any commodity from varying as widely as

[12] A further impairment of the automatic feature would result from use of credit control and tariffs as a supplement to the automatic commodity plan (see pp. 141–143).

[13] The danger of political considerations intervening by these means is readily apparent.

before, but the price fluctuations of any commodity would produce off-setting price fluctuations in some or all of the other commodities.

A question of very great significance concerns the effects upon the general price level and upon the prices of individual commodities and commodity groups comprising this total. Advocates of the plan maintain that the stabilization of the price of the composite unit would operate powerfully in the direction of stabilizing the general price level. It is by no means clear that this result would follow. Experience indicates that the general level of prices may rise at a time when the prices of many basic commodities are unchanged. Movements in the prices of basic raw materials unquestionably will affect the trend of the general price level; but, as long as the plan is designed to affect directly only one segment of the price structure, it seems logical to suppose that the forces now operating to influence prices would not be fully offset. For example, the potentialities of general price movements arising out of security speculation or real estate booms would remain. The adoption of the proposal might not prevent a recurrence of difficulties like those of 1929. But it must be acknowledged that the adoption of the plan would, without much question, prevent a drop as great as that which occurred in the thirties in the price level of the basic commodities included in the monetary unit. This, in turn, might moderate somewhat the decline in the general level of prices; but there is no reason to suppose that a worsening of business conditions such as took place at that time would have been entirely eliminated, unless one holds that the depression was caused solely by the fall in the prices of the basic commodities.

It is quite possible that prices of basic commodities, including those used as the monetary base, might remain stable at a time when other prices were tending to fall (or rise). In such an event, adherence to the commodity reserve currency plan obviously would not assure stability of the general price level. The claim that the proposed plan would guarantee stable prices is based upon the familiar confusion between a general price level and the level of a particular group of prices. It would be fully valid only if it could be assumed that the prices of all commodities outside the monetary unit would behave in precisely the same manner as prices of commodities included in the unit. Commodity currency would contribute to price stability only to the extent that prices of the goods outside the unit followed a pattern identical with those in the unit. It must be concluded that a considerable degree of price fluctuation would be possible under the plan.[14]

[14] The foregoing discussion is not designed to condemn the plan for failing to assure perfection but rather to suggest a tempering of the somewhat extravagant expectations that seem to be cherished by some of its supporters. Cognizance may be taken, also, of other devices such as taxation and fiscal policy, which may be used to regulate price fluctuations. It seems probable, in fact, that these measures may be made

A similar conclusion is reached as to the effect of commodity reserve currency upon secular price movements. Reductions in the real costs of production of all or most of the basic raw materials would tend to lead to a decline in their prices. If it is assumed that, under such conditions, measures are introduced to stabilize the price of the composite unit at the old level, the tendency would be to raise the prices of other commodities whose real costs of production had not declined. An attempt to stabilize the price of the composite unit would, under these circumstances, bring instability to the general price level.

If it is conceded that all segments of the price structure do not necessarily behave in the same manner, it follows that a measure designed to stabilize the price of a group of selected commodities would not necessarily guarantee stability of the general price level, any more than a stable wholesale price level during the twenties resulted in a stabilization of the entire price structure. The stabilization of the price of a group of basic commodities, as provided for by this plan, would not assure stability of the general price level.

The Problem of Credit Control

A further problem suggests itself in connection with the control of credit. The plan would presumably provide for automatic regulation of the supply of basic reserve money. Recent experience with excess reserves has clearly demonstrated, however, that alterations in the volume of reserve money do not guarantee corresponding changes in total credit or even in demand deposits. There is no apparent reason for supposing that experience in this regard would be materially changed by the adoption of the plan.

It is to be noted that the proponents of the plan recognize that the plan does not assure adequate control of credit and that credit may expand or contract independently of changes in basic reserves. They admit the possibility that changes in the supply of commodity reserve currency may be offset by opposite changes in the supply of other forms of money, including demand deposits, or that an inflationary situation may arise unrelated to the new currency. What they fail to point out is that this admission invalidates the claims of automaticity, upon which the case for the plan so largely depends. As an escape from these recognized difficulties a strengthening of present measures for the control of credit has been recommended. It is proposed that all commercial banks be required to join the Federal Reserve System and that the Board of Governors of the Federal Reserve System be given power to fix at its discretion the reserve ratios required of member-banks, on the ground that "no really effective control of our monetary and banking system is possible without these

to provide a quicker and more efficient method of dealing with this problem than that which commodity reserve currency offers.

measures."[15] It is scarcely to be doubted that some such extension of powers is essential to the attainment of the objectives specified in the plan. On the other hand, it may be suggested that, if Congress were willing to grant powers such as these, effective control of credit could probably be secured without the necessity of adopting a commodity reserve currency.

INTERNATIONAL ASPECTS OF THE PLAN

The importance of the international aspects of the plan is generally conceded by its proponents, but, whether intentionally or inadvertently, no attempt has been made to enlarge on the problems involved.[16] The need for further analysis along this line is indicated by the consideration that, unless composite commodity units can perform the function of an international monetary standard as did gold, the analogy with the classic gold standard in its international aspects breaks down.[17]

It seems altogether probable that commodity units having a similar composition are not likely to be adopted as a monetary standard to the same extent as was gold. Yet, unless this were to occur, the commodity reserve money could never fulfil the international function once performed by gold. If similar plans were adopted abroad with the difference that there was a considerable disparity in the proportions given to the individual commodities, the possibility would exist of corresponding divergences in general price movements in the different countries as a result of variations in the prices of the basic raw materials. Failing the establishment of fixed exchange rates, the plan must permit of fluctuating or controlled exchange rates, and thus the gold-standard type of automaticity would be lost.

It has been suggested that, in the event of a drop in world-prices, increased imports into the United States might be accepted in the form of composite commodity units or even of fractional parts of the unit, in exchange for gold, with the desirable result of stimulating business activity abroad and disposing of some of our excessive supply of gold. The sugges-

---

[15] Frank D. Graham, *American Economic Review*, September, 1941, p. 521.

[16] Frank D. Graham states that "the exchange value of a money freely convertible, both ways, in a composite of goods many of which would be freely traded internationally, could not possibly deviate very far from purchasing power parity howsoever computed, and this so far as international matters are concerned, is about all that we can ask." He concludes, however, that "the importance, and especially, the practicability, of stable exchange rates has now ceased to loom as large as it once did in the monetary picture." *American Economic Review Supplement*, March, 1940, p. 15. Similarly, Benjamin Graham states that "since exchange rates are now largely a matter of control and agreement, the question is scarcely relevant to modern conditions." (*Forum on Finance*, p. 187.)

[17] Since gold has now lost its position as an international standard, this hardly bears on the relative merits of the two proposals at the present time.

tion has also been made that changes in the tariff might be employed to influence the importation of commodities included in the unit; in this way it would be possible to influence the quantity of money in circulation. These suggestions raise a number of disconcerting questions. First, even assuming our willingness to accept increased imports for storage purposes, can we assume that other countries would accept gold in exchange at a reasonable valuation? Secondly, to what extent would it become necessary to subordinate our economic foreign policy to the objectives of the plan? Thirdly, is it likely that the monetary authority would be given the requisite degree of control over tariffs? Whatever the answers to these questions, it is self-evident that the advancement of these proposals constitutes an abandonment of the premise of an automatic monetary system. It can scarcely be denied also that the incorporation of such provisions would lay the plan open to grave political abuse.

From an economic standpoint the plan might conceivably be defended as likely to facilitate the repayment of international debts or the discharge of obligations incurred under the Lease-Lend Act. This, however, again involves the question of political feasibility.

IMPLICATIONS FOR AGRICULTURE

In its original formulation the plan proposed not only a sweeping monetary reform but also, in so doing, claimed to present a solution for the farm problem.[18] In recent discussions attention has largely been shifted to the monetary aspects—a fact reflected in the distribution of emphasis in this paper. But the application of the proposal to the farm problem is still significant. Grounds for the belief that the plan would contribute to a solution of the farm problem have already been suggested. It is significant that in a representative year agricultural commodities constitute approximately 70 per cent by value of the commodities included in the unit originally proposed by Benjamin Graham. The adoption of the plan in such form as this would obviously provide a significant demand for certain agricultural commodities, the majority of which are produced in the United States.

It is necessary, however, to consider the present proposal in relation to measures now in force for relieving the farm problem. Such a discussion is called for, first, in order that the relative virtues of this method of aiding agriculture may be evaluated and, secondly, in order that consideration may be given to the possible influence of existing agricultural policies upon the introduction and operation of the plan proposed.

The principal objective of the farm program of the last eight years has been to achieve parity prices for a limited number of farm products.[19]

[18] Benjamin Graham, *Storage and Stability*, p. 169.
[19] Parity prices are the prices at which each farm product included in the program

This objective has been sought through loans and crop reduction. The program is open to criticism on a number of grounds. Stabilization of the prices of individual commodities tends to distort demand and supply relationships. Shifts in production among the favored agricultural commodities and between these commodities and other products are not governed by market considerations alone. The influence of technological changes upon production costs of agricultural products tends to be ignored. The most significant of the criticisms is that the measures now in effect, even though they were first introduced under the guise of an agricultural adjustment act, are uniquely adapted to perpetuate maladjustments both in agriculture as a whole and in particular lines of agricultural production.

The plan for commodity reserve currency, if successful, would assure stability of the price of the composite unit. The prices of the individual commodities included in the unit, on the other hand, would be free to move within limits set by the price of the composite unit. Adjustment to "normal" demand and supply relationships would be possible, and unlimited production of basic agricultural commodities would be discouraged. Provision for the storage of surpluses would allow for the production of commodities in excess of market demand and would serve as a regulator of production to a greater extent than the limited ever-normal granary provided for by existing legislation. The plan, therefore, seems to meet the principal criticisms leveled at the farm program of recent years.

Apart from the relative advantages as judged on purely economic grounds, a rather serious political problem suggests itself. It seems altogether probable that strong opposition would be exerted against replacing present farm legislation by a plan such as is proposed. Even if this did not completely block its introduction, it is quite possible that, for reasons of expediency, an attempt would be made to superimpose the plan on the existing program. If this should happen, the prices of the particular commodities which were guaranteed parity would be relatively fixed. If such commodities were included in the composite unit, the downward rigidity of their prices would greatly hinder, and might make impossible, the satisfactory operation of the commodity reserve currency plan. For existing parity legislation premises a price floor under each of the selected commodities, whereas the proposal under consideration presupposes that prices of the individual commodities will fluctuate about a stable price level of the basic commodities. If the plan were in force, any legislation designed to control prices or production of specific basic raw materials would have greater repercussions than at present on the prices of the individual commodities included in the unit and would subject

would have the same buying power over other products as they had in a previous period. Cotton, wheat, corn, and rice are adjusted to a 1909–1914 price level, tobacco to a 1919–1929 price level.

them to strong pressure by forces other than those of competitive demand and supply. Any measure that succeeded in establishing a high price for any one of the commodities included in the unit would automatically tend to depress the prices of the other commodities through the necessity of maintaining a stable price of the composite unit.

CONCLUSION

The adoption of commodity reserve currency has been advocated as a fundamental reform of our monetary structure. In some of the discussions of the plan the benefits mentioned as likely to accrue from its adoption are presented in terms suggestive of patent-medicine advertising.[20] The analysis presented above has cast doubt on many of the claims advanced. Not only is it questionable whether certain of the advantages would materialize, but, in addition, the transition to commodity reserve currency would assuredly give rise to a troublesome host of new problems.

Many of the advantages claimed for the plan rest upon its fundamental similarity to the gold standard. There is grave reason to fear, however, that placing the basic commodities in the same position as gold, far from preserving all the virtues and none of the vices of the gold standard, would multiply the vices and compromise the virtues of the old gold standard. To concentrate attention on the price level of the basic commodities and the quantity of money is to disregard or minimize the importance of other elements in the price structure. The self-corrective price tendencies envisioned by the proponents of the plan may be admitted; a disturbing feature of the plan lies in the possibility that these tendencies might not become effective until after a considerable maladjustment had taken place.

From the standpoint of practical operation, the plan would be costly. A considerable amount of criticism thus far directed toward the proposal has centered on the costs of storing and handling the basic commodity reserves.[21] No accurate estimates of the costs that might be involved are, of course, possible, although current experience with stock piles and the storage of agricultural surpluses may provide useful data for such calculations.

At the present stage of the discussion, however, consideration of costs would seem to have very little relevance. If further investigation leads to the conclusion that the proposal would produce the effects anticipated

---

[20] "The transition . . . would . . . be not only a painless prophylactic against future evils but also a useful therapeutic for those that were current." (Frank D. Graham, *American Economic Review*, September, 1941, p. 522.) See also the literature of the Committee for Economic Stability.

[21] See especially comments on the plan by Redvers Opie, *American Economic Review Supplement*, 1940, p. 41.

by its proponents, then such costs as might be involved are of minor importance. On the other hand, if it leads to the conclusion that, far from attaining the desired objectives, it would be productive of serious problems, cost considerations are superfluous, clumsy, and confusing as guides for monetary policy and practice. Mention has already been made of the inherent political difficulties and the international complications that would be involved in establishing and maintaining such a system. It is worth remarking that the record of the silver bloc in Congress should be forewarning of the danger of creating a large number of producer groups who would have a pecuniary stake in the monetary standard.

The proponents of the plan acknowledge that the successful introduction and operation of the plan would require many changes in the existing monetary and banking structure. It is not improbable that such changes constitute a considerably sounder and more feasible monetary reform than the adoption of the commodity currency proposal itself. Perhaps the most attractive feature of the entire plan is that it would provide an automatic stimulus to the production of basic commodities when their combined price fell below the coinage value. No corresponding stimulus to production is afforded by present monetary devices. One might look upon the proposal as suggesting a form of self-supporting public expenditure or depression insurance for these commodities. A further attractive feature is that these expenditures would be made automatically without the necessity for governmental appropriations or political maneuvering.

The inadequacy of traditional monetary policy based on the assumed responsiveness of private investment to changes in the supply of credit and interest rates is all too evident from our experience in the thirties. Nevertheless, it is far from clear that the present currency proposal provides the answer that is needed. It could happen that the basic commodity price level was stable, although the general level of prices was depressed. In that case no stimulus would be forthcoming. A more fundamental query arises as to the possible multiplier effects resulting from this plan as compared with various types of public expenditure. Could greater stimulus be expected from these expenditures than from a Muscle Shoals development, a social welfare program, or educational expenditures? It is reasonable to believe that far greater progress toward recovery might be achieved through a selective expenditure program than through the blind encouragement of production in the manner here proposed. And, finally, in view of our experience with gold, it is an alarming and disheartening thought that we should embark upon a plan that calls for the storage of not one but a large number of money commodities.

APPENDIX IV-B

The Critique of Commodity-Reserve Currency: A Point-by-point Reply

BENJAMIN GRAHAM

Reprinted from *The Journal of Political Economy*, Vol. LI, No. 1, February, 1943, pp. 66–69, by permission of the University of Chicago Press and *The Journal of Political Economy*.

In this answer to the article[1] by Messrs. Beale, Kennedy, and Winn, I shall refrain from general comment, except in a brief conclusion. My purpose is to state fairly each one of their objections and either to admit its force or to try to rebut it. It appears best to discuss the various criticisms schematically, in their relation to the claimed advantages of the commodity-reserve proposal.

1. The first benefit asserted is that the commodity-reservoir system will go far to prevent the paradox of want amid plenty by providing an unlimited market at a fair average price for basic commodities as a whole. The expanded purchasing power of the raw-materials producers will greatly stimulate other sectors of the economy.

About this "basic objective" the critique has little to say. It characterizes this "depression-insurance feature" as perhaps the most attractive of the plan; but it suggests that a greater stimulus to general business could be secured "by a selective expenditure program," *e.g.*, on public works. This preference is stated merely as a matter of opinion, without supporting data or argument. Nothing is said as to the economic and political drawbacks of deficit financing or as to the great difficulties of timing and allocation associated with pump-priming. The severe business reaction of 1937–1938 bears testimony to the problems involved. It is easy to stimulate business if the cost is not to be counted—as in war; but this fact alone does not make the case for government spending. (Incidentally, *both* a suitable public works program and a commodity reservoir may prove useful in maintaining full employment.)

2. We claim that the commodity reservoir will constitute an invaluable national asset, useful in emergencies (especially war), for old age pension reserves, and for advancing the living standard.

[1] W. T. M. Beale, Jr., M. T. Kennedy, and W. J. Winn, "Commodity Reserve Currency: A Critique," this *Journal*, L, No. 4, August, 1942, 579–594.

The critique refers to this claim in three scattered passages: (a) it is intimated that the commodity reserves might all be drawn out in a business upswing; (b) the storage of a number of monetary commodities is called "an alarming and disheartening thought" in view of our experience with gold; (c) the possibility of using up the reserve commodities in an emergency is viewed as removing the very protection a monetary reserve is designed to afford.

Taking the last point first, it is obvious that the potential use of the reserve commodities in an emergency cannot possibly be a net disadvantage. If that were so, we should leave them where they are. The option to use them or not must be an advantage; in a war of survival it might be of overwhelming benefit. (England's gold reserve gave her the same kind of advantage in the early years of the war—but only because we were willing to ship commodities in exchange for her gold.)

If it were true that the reserve is likely to be exhausted in good times (by redemption of currency), the plan would operate discontinuously—as, e.g., in the case of a buffer stock of tin. Its effectiveness would be unlimited during declining business, but it might terminate at some point in a boom. We have argued that the commodity reservoir is likely to grow secularly unless special efforts are made to hold it down. The critique does not discuss this point, but its "alarm" at the thought of our gold reserve being imitated by the commodity reserve indicates a similar expectation that the reservoir will grow to large size. Hence, the fear of temporary exhaustion does not appear very realistic.

Would a large supply of reserve commodities be as "disheartening" as our huge accumulation of gold? The objection to our gold hoard is that at bottom it is so useless, especially in wartime. Far from being disheartening, the possession of 22 billion dollars in corn, iron, wool, petroleum, etc., would now be a godsend and possibly our salvation.

3. We contend that the plan will stabilize the price level of basic commodities as a whole and thereby operate powerfully toward stabilizing the general price level.

This assertion is correctly presented at the outset of the critique, but the authors then proceed to argue against an alleged claim that "the proposed plan will guarantee stable prices," i.e., stable prices for everything. Since we make no such pretension, the point need not be pursued.

The critique also seeks to cast doubt on the value of the proposal as a generally stabilizing influence in other price groups—even though it does admit that by preventing a drop in basic commodities, such as in the 1930's, it would "moderate somewhat" the general price decline. It points out that security speculation and real estate booms could not be prevented by our plan. This is true, and I have insisted that extremes in these fields must be avoided by the proper exercise of the Federal Reserve's present powers to control credit.

More seriously, the authors assert that the "commodity currency will contribute to price stability only to the extent that prices of goods outside the unit followed a pattern identical with those in the unit" (p. 587). Surely this stricture goes too far. The Bureau of Labor Statistics data show that important price movements of fabricated goods are invariably blanketed by those of raw materials. The critique advances no reason to doubt our assertion that, if the wide cyclical swings of basic commodities are eliminated, then the swings of finished-goods prices—normally much narrower—will be damped down considerably. This would be even more true of the swings in the price of services (e.g., rents), which are more sluggish than those of goods.

The critique argues that secular price movements will still take place, since the cost and price of other goods may advance vis-à-vis the stabilized unit. Thus the general level, which includes the rising items, will also rise. This possibility will be freely granted as long as it is realized that such price changes are bound to be moderate and nondisturbing. We see no reason to put the whole price level in a straitjacket, and much less to freeze all individual prices. We do say it is essential to hold price fluctuations within tolerable bounds, i.e., to avoid disastrous swings of the 1919–1921, 1930–1933, and 1937–1938 variety. This we believe our plan will accomplish. The critique admits "the self-correcting price tendencies" of the plan but intimates that such tendencies would be delayed "until after a considerable maladjustment has taken place." I fail to find anything said to explain why such a delay should occur. (The reserve mechanism, like the fixed price of gold, does not correct wide fluctuations in the value of the unit; it prevents them.)

In a footnote the authors suggest that the needed degree of price stability could be arrived at more quickly and efficiently by the use of other devices such as taxation and fiscal policy. This is similar to their claim that such measures will afford a better stimulus to depressed business, and, like the other, it is not substantiated by facts or argument.[2]

4. We claim that commodity-reserve currency will be especially sound money, since it would be backed by and convertible into useful goods.

The critique does not mention this claim specifically, nor is it challenged indirectly, except for the criticism that the emergency use of the reserve would destroy the protection which a monetary reserve should supply. This objection has been answered above.

5. We claim that the plan will assist in the settlement of international balances due us by permitting other countries to send us commodity units

---

[2] Other critics of our proposal have asserted that it is better to stabilize individual commodities which need help than to stabilize the unit. Since the critique does not make this point—but rather implies the contrary—I shall not answer it here.

as an alternative to gold. The critique does not deny that international repayments may be facilitated by the plan (p. 590), but it raises an array of objections and "disconcerting questions" in this field, *viz:*

a. International commodity-reserve currency will not produce the gold-standard type of automaticity. Answer: Agreed. This was not claimed. If possible, the international gold standard should be restored, in which case commodity-reserve currency should help its operations. If that is not feasible, the fault lies with the gold standard. We should then have to get along with controlled exchanges, as we have been doing.

b. We might not be able to trade some of our redundant gold for commodity units (as I have suggested), because other nations might refuse to accept gold at a reasonable price. Answer: If so, that would again be the fault of gold. It would demonstrate the superior value of commodity currency over gold currency. Our plan does not depend in any sense on the feasibility of such exchanges.

c. The critique objects to a suggestion of ours that it would be possible to limit the inflow of commodity units by raising tariffs. "Is it likely that the monetary authority will be given the requisite degree of control over tariffs?" Answer: We propose no such monetary authority as the critique seems to envisage. It is not essential to our plan that the inflow of commodity units be controlled, and I should favor accepting all we can get. I merely pointed out that, *if Congress so desired*, Congress would have this means of control available.

d. The critique asks further: "To what extent will it be necessary to subordinate our economic foreign policy to the objectives of the plan?" Answer: To no extent. The three authors have not stated why such subjection should be necessary. They claim, too, that questions of political feasibility will interfere with our accepting commodity units in settlement of foreign debts, but they do not say in what manner. Payments in commodity units need involve no more political questions than payments in gold.

6. We assert that the plan will go far to solve the farm problem by providing an unlimited market for balanced agricultural production. The solution is superior to that of the AAA, because it involves no compulsory curtailment, regimentation, non-recourse loans, or subsidies.

This claim the critique appears to grant (p. 591). But it points out that there would be strong political opposition to replacing present farm legislation by our proposal. Answer: This observation is probably true, even though the economic interests of the farmer are likely to be better served by our provision for balanced abundance than by the AAA's emphasis on scarcity. Properly speaking, however, this is a criticism not of the plan but of those who reject it.

The critique adds that even if the plan were adopted, there would still be political price-fixing of farm commodities, and thus other prices would be disturbed. Answer: If Congress merely held up the price of certain otherwise weak commodities, the result would be to diminish the price advances of other components. This might be inadvisable, but it could scarcely be troublesome. The price of other products would be forced down only if Congress went as far as to push farm prices well *above* their base-period average. Such extreme legislation has not happened before; if there were danger of it, it might be well to have other groups of producers on hand to fight it bitterly as a completely unjustified attack upon their own price structure. One advantage of the interrelationship of prices created by the commodity unit is that an attempt to favor one commodity unduly will promptly and properly create violent opposition by the producers of all the others.

7. On the less dynamic side we assert that our proposal will be self-financing, self-liquidating, and automatic and that the only cost involved will be the relatively small expense of storage. Of these points the critique questions only the claim of automatic action. This is invalidated, it says, by the following nonautomatic provisions: (*a*) periodic revision of the unit, (*b*) possible substitution of futures for spot commodities, (*c*) emergency withdrawal of reserve commodities, (*d*) use of credit control, (*e*) use of tariffs.

Answers: (*a*) Revisions of the unit can be made in accordance with a specific technique laid down in the initial legislation (*Storage and Stability*,[3] pp. 281–82); (*b*) substitutions of futures for spots would also follow a fixed rule and would take place whenever a cash profit could be made thereby; (*c*) emergency withdrawals are an optional (though to my mind a valuable) provision; (*d*) credit control has no organic relationship to our proposal; if it is necessary, that necessity has no bearing on the automatic nature of the commodity-currency mechanism; (*e*) changes in tariffs have been mentioned only as a reminder of the present power of Congress to deal with imports.

SUMMARY

The general conclusions of the critique (which are highly unfavorable) can be valid only to the extent that the individual criticisms are sound. A brief comment on these conclusions may be helpful in the final appraisal. The authors fear that our proposal "would multiply the vices and compromise the virtues of the gold standard." A devastating remark; yet, on the next page they acknowledge that traditional monetary policy, *i.e.*, the gold standard, is inadequate to meet depressions, and they concede that the commodity-reserve mechanism will provide an automatic, self-supporting depression insurance.

A main factor in any evaluation is the relative importance of favorable and adverse elements. The critique admits, in terms, six major advantages

[3] Benjamin Graham, *Storage and Stability*, New York, 1937.

of the plan, *viz:* It will (*a*) hold down price fluctuations in the reserve commodities (p. 586); (*b*) "moderate somewhat" a decline in the general price level (p. 586); (*c*) facilitate repayment of international debts (p. 590); (*d*) meet the principal criticisms leveled at the farm program (p. 591); (*e*) provide an automatic stimulus to raw-materials production in depressions (p. 594); and (*f*) create a stock of basic goods available for emergencies or other uses (p. 585).

Against these benefits it objects that the price stabilization will not be all-pervasive, that the automatic action is not 100 per cent in every sense, that the reserve commodities may be used up in an emergency, etc. Is it not true that all these objections—whatever their accuracy—are of secondary magnitude compared with the primary significance of the benefits which the critics admit? The balance here is not to be struck by an epigram or by vague references to "a troublesome host of new problems." The present writer hopes that this reply will enable the reader to view the merits and shortcomings of the proposal in a sounder perspective than the critique displayed.

APPENDIX IV-C

The Objective of International Price Stability

LORD KEYNES

Reprinted from The Economic Journal, *June–September, 1943, pp. 185–187.*

There are two complaints which it has been usual to lodge against a rigid gold standard as an instrument to secure stable prices. The first is that it does not provide the appropriate quantity of money. This is the familiar, old-fashioned criticism naturally put forward by adherents of the Quantity Theory. The way to meet it is, obviously, to devise a plan for varying appropriately the quantity of gold or its equivalent—for example, the tabular standard of Marshall sixty years ago, the compensated dollar of Irving Fisher forty years ago, or the commodity standard of Professor Hayek expounded in the article printed above.

The peculiar merit of the Clearing Union as a means of remedying a chronic shortage of international money is that it operates through the velocity, rather than through the volume, of circulation. A *volume* of money is only required to satisfy hoarding, to provide reserves against contingencies, and to cover inevitable time-lags between buying and spending. If hoarding is discouraged and if reserves against contingencies are provided by facultative overdrafts, a very small amount of actually outstanding credit might be sufficient for clearing between well-organised Central Banks. The C.U., if it were fully successful, would deal with the quantity of international money by making any significant quantity unnecessary. The system might be improved, of course, by further increasing the discouragements to hoarding.

On another view, however, each national price-level is primarily determined by the relation of the national wage-level to the national efficiency; or, more generally, by the relation of money-costs to efficiency in terms of the national unit of currency. And if price-levels are determined by money-costs, it follows that whilst an "appropriate" quantity of money is a *necessary* condition of stable prices, it is not a *sufficient* condition. For prices can only be stabilised by first stabilising the relation of money-wages (and other costs) to efficiency.

The second (and more modern) complaint against the gold standard is, therefore, that it attempts to confine the natural tendency of wages to rise beyond the limits set by the volume of money, but can only do so by the weapon of deliberately creating unemployment. This weapon the world, after a good try, has decided to discard. And this complaint may be just as valid against a new standard which aims at providing the quantity of money appropriate to stable prices, as it is against the old gold standard.

In the field of price stabilisation international currency projects have, therefore, as I conceive it, only a limited objective. They do not aim at stable prices as such. For international prices which are stable in terms of unitas or bancor cannot be translated into stable national price-levels except by the old gold-standard methods of influencing the level of domestic money-costs. And, failing this, there is not much point in an international price-level providing stability in terms of an international unit which is not reflected in a corresponding stability of the actual price-levels of member countries.

The primary aim of an international currency scheme should be, therefore, to prevent not only those evils which result from a chronic shortage of international money due to the draining of gold into creditor countries but also those which follow from countries failing to maintain stability of domestic efficiency-costs and moving out of step with one another in their national wage-policies without having at their disposal any means of orderly adjustment. And if orderly adjustment is allowed, that is another way of saying that countries may be allowed by the scheme, which is not the case with the gold standard, to pursue, if they choose, different wage policies and, therefore, different price policies.

Thus the more difficult task of an international currency scheme, which will only be fully solved with the aid of experience, is to deal with the problem of members getting out of step in their domestic wage and credit policies. To meet this it can be provided that countries seriously out of step (whether too fast or too slow) may be asked in the first instance to reconsider their policies. But, if necessary (and it will be necessary, if efficiency wage-rates move at materially different rates), exchange rates will have to be altered so as to reconcile a particular national policy to the average pace. If the initial exchange-rates are fixed correctly, this is likely to be the only important disequilibrium for which a change in exchange rates is the appropriate remedy.

It follows that an international currency scheme can work to perfection within the field of maintaining exchange stability, and yet prices may move substantially. If wages and prices double everywhere alike, international exchange equilibrium is undisturbed. If efficiency-wages in a particular country rise ten per cent more than the norm, then it is that there is trouble which needs attention.

The fundamental reason for thus limiting the objectives of an international currency scheme is the impossibility, or at any rate the undesirability, of imposing stable price-levels from without. The error of the gold-standard lay in submitting national wage-policies to outside dictation. It is wiser to regard stability (or otherwise) of internal prices as a matter of internal policy and politics. Commodity standards which try to impose this from without will break down just as surely as the rigid gold-standard.

Some countries are likely to be more successful than others in preserving stability of internal prices and efficiency wages—and it is the off-setting of that inequality of success which will provide an international organisation with its worst headaches. A communist country is in a position to be very successful. Some people argue that a capitalist country is doomed to failure because it will be found impossible in conditions of full employment to prevent a progressive increase of wages. According to this view severe slumps and recurrent periods of unemployment have been hitherto the only effective means of holding efficiency wages within a reasonably stable range. Whether this is so remains to be seen. The more conscious we are of this problem, the likelier shall we be to surmount it.

APPENDIX IV-D

The Objective of Long-term Price Stability

BENJAMIN GRAHAM

The "Comment" of Lord Keynes on Prof. Hayek's article ("A Commodity Reserve Currency," *The Economic Journal*, June–September, 1943, p. 176) was somewhat startling to this writer and to others whom he knows because it appeared to imply that long-term stability in the price level is itself undesirable. The reasoning seemed to be that a steady increase in efficiency-wages (wage cost per unit of output) and hence in selling prices is necessary to prevent recurrent unemployment. Lord Keynes was kind enough to clarify his viewpoint in a personal letter to this writer. The following restatement of Keynes' argument, and the appended discussion, are based on a combination of the published "Comment" and the explanatory letter.

Lord Keynes strongly advocates the suppression of wide short-term fluctuations in prices and favors the use of buffer-stocks of various commodities for this purpose. He believes, however, that the maintenance of a stable *long-term* price level presents problems which a buffer-stock commodity standard—like the gold standard—would have great difficulty in meeting. On this score his argument may be stated as follows:

1. If efficiency-wages should rise substantially the price level would also have to rise even if we had commodity-reserve currency.

2. To make commodity-reserve currency workable for the long term it will therefore be necessary to withstand excessive wage-raising pressure by the trade unions. Some argue that in past practice this has been accomplished only through the experience of unemployment and the fear of it. In this respect commodity-reserve currency would be subject to the same criticism as gold-reserve currency.

3. National policy should try to keep efficiency-wages as stable as it can. This task must consider political as well as economic factors. Here an international system of commodity-backed currency would be objectionable because labor would claim that its wage demands were being opposed—and unemployment created—in deference to international bankers or at least by international dictation.

This reasoning is evidently made up of two quite separate parts. The first relates to the feasibility of long-term price stability in itself. The second deals with the political expediency of an international mechanism for the purpose.

It is true, of course, that a sharp rise in efficiency-wages would make long-term price stability impossible. How real is this danger? Great and constant as has been the advance in money wages during the past 150 years, there is no statistical evidence—in the United States at least—of any underlying tendency for unit costs to rise. The United States has been the leader in wage liberality. As is well known, no secular advance in the wholesale price level is discernible—the pattern being one of recurrent upsurges due to wars followed by a return to former levels.

Will labor now insist that its wages rise faster than efficiency and thus compel a steadily rising price level? This is possible perhaps, but labor union leadership is certainly intelligent enough to recognize that its true interests lie elsewhere. Within the framework of a stable price level three sources of a continued rise in *money wages* may be found: increase in output per hour, reduction in other costs per unit, and reduction in the profit margin paralleling a fall in long-term interest rates. Wage advances beyond these liberal limits are likely to be self-defeating since the resultant price increases may easily lower real wages.

It is also true that a commodity-reserve currency will exert certain pressures to correct wage rises beyond the point compatible with a stable price level. If such advances make it impossible for marginal producers to supply commodity units at their fixed value, a number of these producers will be forced to close down, and thus excessive wage rises will result in some unemployment. This is the type of corrective action which always takes place in our economy; it is a basic competitive factor which in times of peace has operated to keep within reasonable bounds the demands of labor in individual plants and industries.

Yet this corrective shutdown of marginal producers—if it happens—would be by no means the same thing as the recurrent waves of widespread unemployment associated with the trade cycle. The latter flow, in great part, from severe *price declines* which make profitable production impossible even for the efficient firms. The reserve mechanism—buying commodity units at a fixed level—will itself obviate any price collapse of this type. Hence the corrective pressure on wage rises is bound to be comparatively mild and will be relaxed as soon as a viable relationship is reestablished between the fixed price of the commodity unit and the cost of producing it.

It is important to distinguish here, as Prof. Hayek has done, between the employment aspects of the gold standard and of commodity-reserve currency. If the gold standard produces a corrective unemployment, it has no means of checking rapidly the force it sets in motion. It can stimulate employment directly only in the relatively small gold-mining industry. Commodity-reserve currency will offer direct and steady employment to a large segment of the nation's workers provided only that their wage demands are compatible with the price level.

We should add, of course, that the commodity-reserve mechanism will influence directly the prices and wage rates of only the constituent commodities. Theoretically, the wage costs and prices of other commodities and of services could follow an entirely independent pattern. In fact, however, the play of competitive elements is almost certain to result in approximately the same wage and price pattern being followed in the field of finished goods as in that of raw materials. Hence if commodity-reserve currency can maintain both short-term and long-term stability in the price level of basic commodities, it will create indirectly a sufficient degree of stability in other price areas.

Coming to the second aspect of Lord Keynes' argument, if there are political dangers inherent in an international scheme for price-level stability it should not be too difficult to avoid them. Without doubt it is unwise to attempt to impose stability of internal prices from without. As an alternative to adoption of the plan by formal international action, Prof. Hayek has suggested that it would amount in practice to the same thing if it were "operated on the same principle by all the major countries." If the latter method is followed there would be no question of imposing stable prices from without. It is easy to point out that if the United States alone maintained a stable level and if the dollar-bancor rate remains constant, then you have by definition a stable international price level expressed in terms of bancor. Whether this would impose anything on other countries would be a matter of opinion.

In fact this writer is proposing, in a work to be published shortly, that the buffer-stock mechanism be used to stabilize the value of an international commodity unit in terms of bancor, unitas, or United States dollars. If this should be done, it will be for Britain and each other country concerned to decide whether its postwar currency shall have a permanent parity against the commodity unit and the United States dollar. A decision with respect to the dollar-sterling ratio must be made in any case. The problem for Britain should not be made more difficult merely because the United States dollar will have a fixed value in terms of basic commodities. On the contrary, we can scarcely doubt that long-term exchange stability will be more easily achieved if long-term prices of world commodities are stable than if they are unstable.

INDEX

Recommended Readings

- Technical Analysis of Stock Trends, Robert D. Edwards, John Magee, www.bnpublishing.net

- Wall Street: The Other Las Vegas, Nicolas Darvas, www.bnpublishing.net

- The Anatomy of Success, Nicolas Darvas, www.bnpublishing.net

- The Dale Carnegie Course on Effective Speaking, Personality Development, and the Art of How to Win Friends & Influence People, Dale Carnegie, www.bnpublishing.net

- The Law of Success In Sixteen Lessons by Napoleon Hill (Complete, Unabridged), Napoleon Hill, www.bnpublishing.net

- It Works, R. H. Jarrett, www.bnpublishing.net

- Darvas System for Over the Counter Profits, Nicolas Darvas, www.bnpublishing.net

- The Art of Public Speaking (Audio CD), Dale Carnegie, wwww.bnpublishing.net

- The Success System That Never Fails (Audio CD), W. Clement Stone, www.bnpublishing.net

www.ingramcontent.com/pod-product-compliance
Lightning Source LLC
Chambersburg PA
CBHW030651270326
41929CB00007B/308